Write as an Expert

Write as an Expert

Explicit Teaching of Genres

Liz Simon

HEINEMANN
Portsmouth, NH

Heinemann

A division of Reed Elsevier Inc.

361 Hanover Street

Portsmouth, NH 03801–3912

www.heinemann.com

Offices and agents throughout the world

Library of Congress Cataloging-in-Publication Data

Simon, Liz.

    Write as an expert : explicit teaching of genres / Liz Simon.

       p. cm.

    Includes bibliographical references.

    ISBN 0-325-00685-7 (alk. paper)

    1. Literature—Study and teaching (Elementary). 2. Literary form—Study and teaching (Elementary). I. Title.

LB1575.S517 2004

372.62'3—dc22   2004017187

Editor: Lois Bridges

Production: Lynne Costa

Cover design: Catherine Hawkes, Cat & Mouse

Cover photograph: Liz Simon

Typesetter: Valerie Levy/Drawing Board Studios

Manufacturing: Steve Bernier

Printed in the United States of America on acid-free paper

09 08 07 06 05 VP 1 2 3 4 5

To my sweeties, Eloise, Jesse, and especially Ben,
whom we almost lost this year.

CONTENTS

Some educators are passionate about children learning the structures and language of writing genres. Some educators are not. Here's what teachers in Jersey City, New Jersey, had to say after they implemented a unit on report writing in their classrooms:

> [The children] are not complaining. Everyone is involved because they like the topic—animals—and they like the structure. They are focused on one thing at a time.
>
> —Bridget Cullen, first-grade teacher

> It worked. In this class we have ESL and special education students who are able to write their own reports from key words. The children's confidence has improved. Their writing is more accurate, and they are writing faster than before.
>
> —Camille Garison and Marcia Hernandez, second-grade teachers

Figure 1 on page x shows an example.

And one of the students had this to say:

> I have been learning more about animals—the elephant is perfect. Getting in touch with animals was interesting. There is a pattern I know when I write and when I write I feel I am learning more.

When I first began teaching, the children in my class started out by writing about their personal experiences: *I went to the beach.* As the year progressed, they began to create imaginative adventures: *The boy met a monster and they walked down the street and*

February 25, 2004 ROUGH DRAFT

Dinosaurs

My report is about dinosaurs.

Dinosaurs are reptiles.

~~There~~ *There* were some dinosaurs that ~~have~~ *had* big heads and sharp teeth. Some dinosaurs ~~have~~ *had* long necks and very long bodies.

They're some dinosaurs that ~~have~~ *had* thick armor and spikes on *their* tails with horns.

There *were* even ~~creches~~ *creatures* that looked, like birds looked like birds and had feathers. ⓒ $\frac{25}{?}$ *difficulty with* ~~*tenses*~~

Dinosaurs lived it was warm and wet. Some creatures ate tropical plants while others eat gidnt fern. Most dinosaurs eat meat, plant, leaves, insects, lizards and tops of trees. Lots of dinosaurs ran fast or slow.

I hope you like my report about dinosaurs did *you* learn anything!

found an old coat. The boy said to the monster "You have the coat" and the monster said "Yes." They went home. The end. The pieces were either short, in which case I told them, "Write more," but didn't show them how (I don't think I knew), or long discourses, often repetitive, often unstructured. I was sure there had to be a better way.

And then I discovered genres. When I began to plan for and implement lessons on various specific genres, the writing in my classroom became exciting. Children began writing longer pieces; their writing was structured and had more meaning. The language they used was far more interesting and creative. I was thrilled.

After my initial experimentation, I planned a whole year around teaching selected writing genres, spending five weeks or more on an in-depth study of each one. (When my students knew very little about a genre, I extended the time in order to include more activities at the point of writing.) What an amazing year. The quality and creativity of the writing the children produced were wonderful. My students became confident writers; by learning the structures and language of each genre, they were able to make informed decisions about their writing and become expert writers.

I hope reading this book will stimulate you to implement the teaching of writing genres in your own classroom.

ACKNOWLEDGMENTS

I have read so many authors' works on writing genres—too many to remember and acknowledge personally. But I would like to thank them as a group for inspiring me, many years ago, to attempt a writing genre program in my classroom and for continuing to broaden my knowledge about writing genres.

I would like to thank math consultant Kathy Smythe for the math problem she suggested. To the children who contributed their work: I want to express my gratitude to you. And Sandi Hawke, I still have the comparison poem your children wrote about me. Finally, I want to thank my daughter, Alicia, for the many ideas she has given me, and my husband, Tony, for being so patient as I sat at the computer morning, noon, and night.

Once again I am indebted to Lois Bridges, Lynne Costa, Alan Huisman, and others from Heinemann for their professionalism and high-quality editing and production of my book. It is wonderful to be associated with such a friendly and encouraging team.

What's a Genre?

The term *genre* is associated with literature, music, and art and defines a category of things within those artistic forms that have the same general characteristics. Genres are socially and culturally determined. For example, publishers of storybooks tend to list them under broad headings such as fiction, expository nonfiction, narrative nonfiction, and so on. When we write in a particular genre, we follow a structure associated with that kind of literature, using certain linguistic forms to communicate a particular purpose.

I often get into arguments when I discuss writing genres with other educators. Someone tells me, "The children observed their dog and wrote what they observed: 'Our dog eats biscuits.' That is a report." However, it seems more like a recounting to me. Or someone else states firmly, "A response should be considered an expository piece of writing." Indeed, according to the definition of expository writing—"setting forth facts and/or ideas point by point; interpreting and/or clarifying"—responses, explanations, and reports can all be considered examples of it.

I feel that children should initially be exposed to recognizable examples of writing genres that have a particular function (purpose) and audience. Except for poetry, the genres in this book all have a similar structure: an orientation, an expansion of the orientation, and a closure. What makes each genre recognizable is the content and the language through which that content is expressed.

What Are the Elements of Genre?

Writing genres comprise relationships between context, text, and language:

- The subject matter, the content or meaning *recognizable through the language of the text,* is referred to as the *field.* It is what is being written about in a particular context or from a particular perspective. For example, I recognize the following piece of writing as persuasive exposition because of its content (it's promoting travel to Canada) and its emotive language (the value judgments and slogans): *This winter when you're looking for an escape that will set your spirit soaring, look to Canada. Here you'll discover an international destination. . . . Discover true nature with an unforgettable trip to Canada.*

- The form of the language, either as part of the action or as a reflection of it, is referred to as the *mode.* It is the role language plays in making meaning: how language is structured and what words are chosen. For example, from the factual statements and the technical words used, I recognize the following writing as a report; it imparts information about owls: *Owls hunt by night for small prey. They are nocturnal. . . . They depend on camouflage.*

- The mood, or *tenor,* of the piece refers to how the story is told. The tenor can range from *informal language* (which sounds more like speaking, as in a social letter, for example) to the *formal, explicit language* of exposition. The tenor of the language depends on the role of the writer and his relationship with his audience: a social letter written to Dad, an exposition written for a formal presentation.

Why Teach Writing Genres?

It is expected that children will be taught to write "texts associated with daily life" (social letters, for example) as well as "specialized texts" (exposition, for example) and that within these contexts "there is a standard variety of English, distinguishable by its grammar and vocabulary. . . . Students' use of linguistic structures and features will vary according to their purpose [and] topic. . . . Proficient language users choose the most appropriate mode of communication, the most effective textual patterns, words, grammatical structures and stylistic features" (Curriculum Corporation 1994).

Children's writing needs to progress from the informal *I went to the shops and I bought a toy* to the formal *Mercury is the planet closest to the Sun.* By teaching children to write in the various genres, we better equip them to participate in all areas of the curriculum, at all educational levels, and to follow any future career path they wish to take. By helping children observe, research, and become experts on a topic and its related language (field), learn about the language and linguistic structures of genres (mode), and use more formal language (tenor), we support their ability to function in the world by giving them the skills to be able to write in the forms common to the cultures of school and society.

Teaching genre formats helps children develop these skills:

- Observing: looking closely, describing what they see
- Listening: participating in games and activities
- Remembering: recapping what they have learned
- Questioning: asking themselves questions
- Thinking: considering alternatives
- Transferring: using the things they've learned about one genre when writing in another
- Cooperating: working in groups

Teaching Genres Explicitly

When children are taught genre formats, they are able to use explicit language when talking about the schemas or language associated with these formats (the *where, when, who, what,* and *how* of narrative, for example). Explicit teaching makes learning accessible to every child, especially children who find learning difficult, because it eliminates confusion. Explicit teaching lets children in on the *secrets* of how learning in the classroom is achieved and what strategies a learner uses to learn; each child is given the utmost chance to be successful.

As the term implies, explicit teaching relates directly to how knowledgeable a teacher is about learning outcomes, the explicit language needed to achieve them, and the most suitable teaching methods and activities that allow children to learn and practice an aspect of curriculum. Teachers need to learn about a particular writing genre—its field, tenor, and mode—before they can teach it.

The framework presented in this book is very precise and employs teaching methods and language that give explicit messages. Through intense study, children

- Understand and internalize different genres and their characteristics
- Understand why particular genres are used for particular communicative purposes
- Recognize slight genre variations

Not only are the children told things explicitly, given demonstrations, questioned, helped to deconstruct texts, and helped to construct writing in shared sessions, but they also consistently participate in discussions and activities that expand their knowledge and vocabulary. These activities reinforce and allow them to practice the new processes, schemas, and language structures they will need when they write independently.

Planning

Writing genre instruction requires two types of planning: global and developmental.

- Global planning:
  - Planning the genres to be studied for the year (see the Writing Genres Developmental Framework on page 14)
  - Continuously planning, over a period of time, distinct and comprehensive learning outcomes that relate to a particular genre being studied
- Developmental planning: Planning how to teach a writing genre, beginning with a simple concept and gradually building on that knowledge, allowing each child to work at his or her developmental level. This kind of planning takes into account individual children's skills and maturity. Therefore, developmental planning involves
  - Purposefully planning a teaching and learning focus for the day, including questions to be asked, techniques that need to be modeled, and activities that allow knowledge and understanding to develop
  - Telling children the intended outcome for the day, which allows children to internalize the particular learning aspect

Modeling

Modeling is a matter of *how* teachers impart their knowledge of writing genres to students. Direct interaction like this is not vague or fuzzy: the teacher has in mind definite teaching and learning focuses and deliberately imparts this knowledge to the children.

The role of *reading* and *deconstructing text* is most important. Reading a variety of texts aloud to children of all ages will bring texts alive for them and will attract their attention to the structures, ideas, themes, writing styles (how authors manipulate words to achieve particular effects), and language in literary pieces. Published text—fictional and informational big books, picture books, novels, poems, newspapers—"moves [children] out of their personal language into other areas of language; [they] access language that is beyond their normal range" (Barrs 2000).

Teacher-directed discussions and activities in which texts are deconstructed (isolated into parts) help children

- Become aware of the characteristics of the different genres
- Critically examine and compare text and language structures of different genres
- Understand the circumstances for writing particular genres—their purposes and their audiences
- Comprehend texts—make connections with prior knowledge; predict; make comparisons; visualize; make inferences; determine the important facts; question; summarize; and develop ideas, judgments, and understanding based on information in the text

Children need to be made aware that they can incorporate in their own writing literary techniques, schemas, language structures, and graphic elements that they have encountered in established texts.

Constructing text in front of the children during shared writing expands children's field knowledge and their ability to use language independently. Children

- Become aware of *strategies* they can use—making links to other genres, innovating on literary pieces, linking new spelling to words they know. While text is being constructed, students and teacher discuss ideas, find ways to solve problems, and carefully attend to and analyze print.
- Learn about schemas and language structures.

- Take what is appropriate to their particular thinking and language developmental level.
- Are able to make informed choices in their own writing, gradually incorporating new language structures.

Any number of things can be modeled during the joint construction of texts:

- Text:
  - Using strategies to assist understanding: predicting, connecting new information to prior knowledge, inferring, asking questions, visualizing, summarizing and combining these elements (synthesizing) to develop new ideas, judgments, and understanding
  - Composing genre structures: varied ways to begin narratives, for example
  - Innovating: adding new verses, manipulating words
  - Recapturing the sense of a written piece by rereading
  - Planning: outlining beginnings, events, endings
  - Linking genres with similar characteristics
  - Using question maps or lists to help solve problems (Children are able to take responsibility for solving problems and to act on their understanding.)
- Language:
  - Structuring sentences: clauses (a group of words with a subject, something said about the subject [predicate], and a finite verb); phrases connecting ideas (text cohesion); placement of capital letters; punctuation (periods, commas, quotation marks, exclamation points, question marks); *Father and I*; *a, an*; creating compound sentences through the use of conjunctions; and so on
  - Being aware of spacing—the white parts between words
  - Using descriptive language: adjectives, verbs, adjectival phrases, adverbial phrases
  - Grammar: verb tenses, *-ed* and *-ing* endings, plurals, possessives
  - Paragraphing and using headings
- Words:
  - Extending vocabulary by using synonyms to vary writing
  - Spelling: homonyms (*to, too, two; their, there*), digraphs, blends, syllables, prefixes, suffixes, contractions

- Checking spelling: spelling question map, circling words to check later in the dictionary
- Using a dictionary: alphabetical order, word meanings, word forms
- Other:
  - Letter formation
  - Publishing—editing and revising
  - Finding resources and equipment in the room

Using Activities at the Point of Writing

Quite often children simply do not know what cognitive or procedural steps to take as they prepare to write. They need to participate in discussions and activities through which they learn the language related to exploring and making sense of a topic—terms like *classification, description, definition, comparison*, and *generalization*. If they become knowledgeable about the topic and learn to use particular processes, thinking strategies, and language, they will write better and more easily.

For example, *role playing* allows children to experience a character's reactions and feelings, helps them identify more fully with the character, and gives them a better understanding of the character's actions and relationships. Additionally, on a more technical level, they can be shown how adverbs, conjunctions, and prepositions formalize writing. After participating in these activities, they will be more adroit and inventive when describing a character's role in a story or arguing a point related to an issue.

Using Inquiry

Inquiry is a challenging way of allowing children to set "directions and actively participate in the construction of learning experiences" (Short, Burke, and Harste 1996). In inquiry, information and understanding are pursued by way of questions that are stimulated during the construction of shared knowledge.

For example, children could begin building knowledge about the recounting genre by reading and examining lots of storybooks with this question in mind: *How do authors make stories?* As they explore and investigate lots of different texts in order to solve the puzzle of how stories are made, they sustain and extend their learning by asking more specific questions: *This author began the story with the* main character saying, *"I wonder if it could be true?"* Why did the author begin this way?

Inquiry is also a supportive way to work with the report and exposition genres. Rather than announcing, *We are studying plants*, the teacher formulates a significant, open-ended, nonjudgmental question: *Are plants important?* This draws children's attention toward universal themes or issues. Then, before beginning their research or investigation, the children can build shared knowledge by taking a field trip to a botanical garden or reading a big book about plants. They begin to discover things that puzzle them or that they want to know more about; they "find questions that are significant to the learner" (Hamster and Murdoch 2000). Once children have asked and prioritized these questions, children can use them to research and investigate the universal theme systematically.

Writing

Children who write gain a lot of expertise in all aspects of the writing process. Children need to write every day and for reasonable lengths of time. The environment should be quiet so they can concentrate (especially at the beginning of the session).

But some children may either need more support or be reluctant to write independently. Here are some ways to help them.

Interactive Writing

This form of supportive writing is especially effective for introducing the writing process to new or unsure writers. With teacher support, a small group of five or six children suggest ideas and share the same pen to construct the text.

First the children think of an idea (generally stimulated by their own experiences, a published text, or shared writing), and then each takes a turn writing related words or parts of words on a large sheet of paper or a medium-size board. As they do so, they learn left-to-right directional behavior, learn to begin sentences with capital letters and finish them with periods, learn to leave spaces between words, and learn spelling strategies (e.g., hearing sounds in words).

Guided Writing

Guided writing for small groups is a technique that not only supports reluctant and delayed older writers but also extends more able writers' thinking, inventiveness, and linguistic expertise. The children in a guided writing session use their own pens and writing books. Text is constructed both jointly and independently. The teacher

- Determines a genre-related teaching and learning focus for the group.
- Guides the writing: *What aspect of this genre are we working on? What information do we need to include?*
- Prompts the group to reread their written piece and improve it. Specific ways to do this include:
  - Showing how the plot needs to unfold or how to build tension.
  - Asking questions: *Does this sound right? Should it be past tense?*
  - Demonstrating a particular spelling strategy.
  - Demonstrating adding an adjective before a key noun.
  - Placing capital letters at the beginning of new sentences and periods at the end of sentences.
- Asks the children to articulate what they have learned during the lesson.
- Has the children continue the writing task independently.

Paired Talking and Writing

Older children generally respond well to talking and writing with a partner. This can be done with peers but also with older-younger teams. The schematic in Figure 2 is based on Keith Topping and colleagues' "Paired Writing: A Framework for Effective Collaboration" (2002).

Holding Conferences

During conferences, the teacher and individual children (or small groups) work together to improve the children's writing. Together, they talk about ways to extend ideas and enliven the writing, looking at other ways to express things. Prompts include: *Would it be useful for you to . . . ?* and *You may want to . . .*

Conferences should be conducted every day in a quiet area in the classroom. Both the teacher and the child (or children) have a joint focus:

- *Asking* an open-ended question: *What are you trying to do today?*
- *Listening* to the child's thoughts about aspects of his or her writing.

Figure 2

Paired Talk-and-Write Process					
1. Planning/ Ideas	**2. First Draft**	**3. Read**	**4. Edit**	**5. Best Copy**	**6. Evaluate**
Discuss these questions: What will the title be? How do we begin? What next? How will it end? *Draw a story map.* *Reread your ideas.*	*Refer to your story map and, together, write down and sequence your ideas.* Don't worry about spelling or punctuation *but* make your writing legible and use clear spacing.	*Read the rough draft aloud to each other.* Check meaning and change if necessary.	*Discuss and improve.* Use a colored pencil to make changes. *Ask yourselves these questions when you reread your work:* First reading: Does it sound right? Second reading: Are there incorrect spellings? (circle them and check the dictionary later) Third reading: Is the punctuation correct?	*Rewrite if necessary, incorporating all corrections.*	*Read your finished work and comment.* What do we think? What next?

- *Looking* at aspects of the child's writing. (It is not necessary to read the whole piece.)
- *Making a teaching decision* that focuses on one learning point (in genre studies, the focus is often the teaching point for that day or week):
  - Extending thinking, complexity of sentences, or problem-solving strategies.
  - Making relationships between new learning and learning secured or almost secured.
  - Revealing confusions.

- Rereading to determine whether ideas are sequentially stated.
- Examining writing to see whether adding some adjectives would enhance the imagery.
- Describing characters or a scene more fully.
- Discussing the importance of limiting characters. Are new characters introduced halfway through the story and the original characters never mentioned again?
- Concentrating on punctuation. Are there capitals at the beginning of sentences and periods at the end of sentences?
- Discussing the research, the notes that have been taken.
- *Setting a goal.* The child sets a goal to work on during independent writing.

A Writing Conference Record (see BLM 41, page 173), helps teachers keep a brief record of the interactions.

How This Book Is Organized

Each chapter discusses a different genre, in the following format:

1. The function or purpose of the genre, followed by a program plan (schematic) that lists the text structures, language structures, and conventions to be taught. (BLM 39 on page 171 is a blank Program Plan.)
2. Implementation details, beginning with simple concepts and gradually building to more complex ones.
3. A Learning Outcomes Profile on which to state each child's progress in achieving the learning outcomes to be expected from the program plan. (BLM 40 on page 172 is a blank Learning Outcomes Profile.) When children have completed a genre study, this outcomes profile, along with a piece of writing, becomes part of the report package provided to their parents. Copies can also be forwarded to next year's teacher. (Assessment of research or experimentation genres—reports, explanation, exposition—is ongoing.)

Rather than compartmentalize the teaching of genres into grade levels, I have targeted the information and activities for *early, transitional,* and *extending* writers, since most primary classes will include some of each. (I do not deal with emergent writers here. For an approach to working with these writers, see my 2004 book *Strategic Spelling: Every Writer's Tool,* Chapter 1.)

A Writing Genres Developmental Framework is presented on page 14. In addition to the usual genres (narrative, poetry, fiction, reports), this framework includes

- *Explanation,* which concentrates on mathematics learning journals, in which children explain the processes they use when solving mathematical problems. Writing an explanation helps them clarify their mathematical thinking.
- *Media news report* and *Exposition.* The newspaper epitomizes our cultural literacy and could be described as a cultural artifact. It is a resource for learning about real life. Media news reports and Exposition letters to the editor, articles, and the like are primarily for *extending* writers.

Assessments are generally performed at the end of each genre study. In a quiet environment, for a predetermined length of time (that is, under "test" conditions), children write independently to show their understanding of the genre they have just studied. The teacher then analyzes this writing in relation to the Learning Outcomes Profile and forms judgments about the students' achievements. The expectation is that children's linguistic ability and vocabulary will increase with each genre studied.

Preteaching Organizational Habits

Before beginning a writing genre program, it's a good idea to teach children to be more organized and focused during writing sessions. There is always some child who hasn't got a pencil or the correct book. This gets the session off to a slow start and distracts the unprepared child from the objective of the lesson. Children are more responsible for their equipment if each one has a pencil case and their books are clearly labeled.

It's also helpful to model getting equipment from a *tidy* storage area. Make rules together aimed at keeping the storage area neat. Model how to get out pencils and books and sit on the carpet quickly, and have the children practice this every day for a week. At the beginning of each writing session, ask children what they did to get organized. Praise and incentives like gold stars work wonders.

A poster that shows explicitly in pictures and symbols how to pre-pare for writing is a very effective tool (see Figure 3).

Figure 3

Figure 4

Writing Genres Developmental Framework

Early	Transitional	Extending
Writing is primarily informal, speechlike (with some formal elements)	*Writing is more formal than speechlike*	*Formal writing*
Poetry: Free verse	Poetry: Cumulative, rhyming	Poetry: Rhyming (limericks) Imagery (alliteration, onomatopoeia, simile) Haiku, cinquain*
Message: A card, for example ("Dear Mom")*	Letter: Social	Letter: Impersonal*
Recounting: Personal happenings ("I went . . .") A story ("The brown bear could see a horse") (only mentioned)	Recounting: Personal happening (a particular experience, a narration) Story (orientation, middle [problem, solution], end) Biography*	Recounting: Historical*
Response to literature: Drawing, writing Reason (because) (only mentioned)	Fiction: Imaginative story (children's own creations) Adventure, fantasy (orientation, middle [problem, solution], end)	Fiction: Adventure, fantasy (more content, description, cause, effect, climax) Fables*, science fiction* Plays*
Report: Simple information (only mentioned)	Response to literature: Reviews	Response to literature: Reviews Reading logs, literature circles
Procedure: Recipe* How to make something* How to grow things*	Report: Information, animal Event* (field trip, for example)	Report: Information (various topics) Inquiry-based (research) Cause-and-effect (storms, for example)* Contrast (lifestyles of Iroquois and early immigrants, for example)* Media news
	Procedure: Science experiment*	
	Explanation: Math journals Phenomenon*	Explanation: Math journal Phenomenon*
	Exposition: Persuasion (advertisement)	Exposition: Persuasion (letter to the editor, article) Argument and counterargument

* not included in this book

Poetry

The function of poetry is to share language as an art form.

—Michelle Anstey

Poems engage our emotions and our sense of wonder and fun.
Words and ideas play together within the patterns of rhythm
and rhyme.

—Susan Hill

There are many different types of poetry, arranged in many different patterns on the page. A common attribute of poetry is that it is very descriptive and causes the reader to form mental pictures, or *images*. Poetry also reveals emotion. Common poetic devices are rhyming, alliteration, onomatopoeia, and simile.

Poetry in this genre framework begins with repetitive-pattern free verse. Early writers learn to innovate on existing poems. Children use repetitive nouns in *cumulative verse* (approximately five lines). They also learn about placing adjectives in front of nouns to create images. (Using adjectives to expand and enliven writing is part of each succeeding genre.)

Children are introduced to rhyme through innovations on established poems with the AA rhyming pattern. Limericks are explored, as are poems that use alliteration, onomatopoeia, and simile.

You can provoke children's imagination by asking them to close their eyes and *see* a boy accidentally sitting on a plate of chocolate cupcakes, *hear* the long grass rustling in the wind, *taste* drops of rain, *touch* with

Figure 5

Poetry Program Plan
Free verse (early writers)
Cumulative verse (transitional writers)
Rhyme (transitional and extending writers)
Imagery (extending writers)

Content
Free verse, repetitive phrases
Cumulative verse
Rhyme: innovations, chants, nursery rhymes
Limericks
Imagery: alliteration (acrostic poems), onomatopoeia, simile
Paintings and poetry

Text Structures	Language Structures	Conventions
Each idea on a new line	Using verbs	Using the initial capital
	Using rhyming words	Using the final period
		Using the comma
Repeated phrases		Using the exclamation point
Cumulative verse, increasing the number of words on each line (end of line remains a noun)	Creating imagery using adjectives, adverbs, alliteration (words beginning with the same sounds), onomatopoeia (words representing animal or environmental sounds), simile (comparison sentences using *like* and *as*)	
AA rhyming pattern		
Limerick (five lines, AABBA)		
Imagery: alliteration, onomatopoeia, simile		

Activities at the Point of Writing
Listen to and read lots of different poems: rhyming couplets, rhythmic verse, songs, poems
Compare poems with big books written in prose
Innovate on an existing poem by changing phrases and key words (publish a big-book version for the class)
Read a poem and have children draw or paint the images evoked
Establish the concept of adjectives and where they appear in sentences
Label pictures with adjectives
Go for a walk and have children lie on the ground, close their eyes, and use their senses to stimulate feelings, emotions
Use a Kid Pix® computer program to write and draw
Recite poems
Invite a painter or poet to visit the classroom

their feet something furry and warm at the bottom of the bed, or *smell* the frying bacon. Explain that *poetic license* allows the normal rules of language to be bent.

If children are to write poetry, they need to be shown examples. There are many interesting poets, especially contemporary ones, for children to study. Read lots of poems together, both to enjoy them and to show how poetry really works. Reading poems aloud, emphasizing how words are manipulated to achieve particular effects, helps children develop a sense of the way language triggers mental images. Comparisons between prose and poetry (prose is not written in verse form) are also helpful.

As children write in a variety of poetic styles (haiku and cinquain, for example), they learn terms like *verse* (a line of metrical language), *couplet* (a pair of verses of the same metrical length that form a unit), and *stanza* (a group of lines forming a division within a longer poem).

During this unit, you can publish big books for the classroom—children can key the text on the computer and add illustrations, either computerized or hand-drawn. The children can publish small books of poems they have written. They love to see their work in print. They can also share their creative work with other classes.

Lead-In

Introduce the poetry genre by reading lots of chants, rhymes, and poems, and have children act them out or clap or skip as they recite them with you.

Free Verse: Repetitive Phrases

Free verse does not rhyme but may have rhythm. Sentences may vary in length.

Begin by reading the short rhythmic verse "I Like . . ." to the children.

I Like . . .
I like sausages
I like stew,
I like me,
I like you.

I like ice cream
And chocolate, too.
I like me
And I like you.

Then share with the students as you and they write a similar repetitive verse:

> I like doughnuts,
> I like fish,
> I like pudding
> In a dish.

Finally, have children write their own short verses.

➥ Here are some more examples of verses from which you can extract a phrase that children can innovate on in order to create repetitive free verse:

> I love noodles,
> Give me oodles,
> Make a mound up to the sun.
> Noodles are my favorite foodles,
> I eat noodles by the ton.

Phrase to innovate:

> *I love . . .* or *I eat . . .*

> Bobby met a beetle,
> A big black beetle, too!
> But Bobby, being brave and bold,
> Cried, "Boo, Beetle, boo!"

Phrase to innovate:

> *. . . met a . . .*

> Here is a feather,
> It belongs to a bird.
> Here is a branch,
> It belongs to a tree.
> Here is a shell,
> It belongs to a snail.
> And here is a smile,
> It belongs to me.

Phrase to innovate:

> *Here is a . . .*
> *It belongs to a . . .*

> I dream I am a driver
> And I drive a speedy train,
> I dream I am a pilot
> And fly a big jet plane,
> I dream and I dream
> Of lots of things to be,
> But when it comes to morning time
> I find that I am me.

Phrase to innovate:

> *I dream I am . . .*

➥ While maintaining the repetitive element, extend the writing of free verse. Read a repetitive story like *Five Little Monkeys,* by Eileen Christelow (1991; "Five little monkeys jumping on the bed . . ."), and have the children, in pairs, use the same pattern to write their own poems. (This is a good time to look at singular and plural noun forms: the *-s* at the end of a word.) Here is one innovation on the story:

> Five big koalas jumping in a tree
> Four floppy koalas jumping in a tree
> Three grey koalas jumping in a tree
> Two fluffy koalas jumping in a tree
> One quiet big koala sitting in a tree.

Have the children publish their free verse poems as small books to place in the library or take home.

➤ Write the poem from *Brown Bear, Brown Bear, What Do You See?* (Martin 1992) in large print. Read the poem and then let the children innovate on the text (they could change the color, the type of animal, what the animal does). Write the innovations on sticky notes or white correction tape placed over the original text. Later, publish a big book and let the children add illustrations.

> Black seal, black seal, what do you eat?
> Orange spider, orange spider, what do you eat?

➤ Have children, in pairs, look out the classroom window or door and see what they can see:

> Ali and Destiny, what can you see?
> We can see a bleak yard,
> No children at all.

➤ Read the big book *Zoo-Looking*, by Mem Fox (1996), and innovate on it:

"She looked at the giraffe and the giraffe looked back."	He listened to the wind and the wind whispered back.
	He listened to the rain and the rain splashed back.
(Last line)	
	He listened to the bear as it crept around the sack.

Other repetitive formats (Dillon and Cahill 1991) include

Hello . . . , goodbye . . .
I used to . . . , but now I . . .
I see . . .
I hear . . .
I touch . . .
I taste . . .
I smell . . .

Cumulative Verse: Introducing Adjectives

➥ First establish whether the children know what adjectives are (adjectives describe a noun). Then read the story *Our Granny*, by Margaret Wild (1993). Afterward, *find and list the nouns* in the story. Again explain what an adjective is, and then *find and list the adjectives* in front of the nouns:

thin legs	*crinkly* eyes	*silky* dresses
fat knees	*friendly* smiles	*big* bras
bristly chins	*big, soft* laps	*saggy* underpants
interesting hair		

You could make a game for the literacy learning center in which children must match adjectives with pictures of the nouns they modify.

"The House that Jack Built" (Taback 2002) and "There Was an Old Lady Who Swallowed a Fly" (Taback 1997) are cumulative poetry forms that help children gradually form images in their minds; images that are repeated and gradually keep expanding. Beginning with the fly being swallowed by the old woman, to the unbelievable—a horse being swallowed by the old woman—also introduces children to cause and effect (and, of course, humor!).

➥ You can introduce another form of cumulative poetry that assists childrens' use of adjectives. Write a poem you create yourself on graph paper. Think of an animal and gradually begin to describe the animal, for example, "The Tiger," written by the author (unpublished). This poem gives vivid descriptions of a tiger lying in wait for its prey. The children could close their eyes and see the images.

The Tiger

The crouching tiger lies in wait,
The crouching, silent tiger lies in wait,
The orange-coated, crouching, silent tiger lies in wait,
The black-striped, orange-coated, crouching, silent tiger lies in
    wait,
The twitching-eared, orange-coated, black-striped, crouching,
    silent tiger lies in wait.

His coal-black eyes are shining bright
His horny nails begin to catch the light
Making ready to give his prey and awful fright!

Read the poem again and deconstruct the text by deleting many of the descriptive words. Again, ask the children to close their eyes as you read the altered poem.

The tiger lies in wait
His eyes are bright,
His nails begin to catch the light
Making ready to give his prey a fright!

Ask which poem creates the best images and why. Then read the poem again and reinstate all those wonderful adjectives that give the reader mental images.

While you read "The Tiger" aloud, have the children make drawings on small chalkboards, whiteboards, or paper. They should produce some wonderful crouching, silent tigers!

➨ Read *The Rainbow Fish,* by Marcus Pfister (1995). The first time, just have the children listen. As you read the story a second time, list the adjectives from the text: *deep, blue, green, purple, sparkling silver.* Model writing a cumulative poem using the adjectives. Draw a large fish on a sheet of paper and in large print write adjectives the children suggest to describe the fish.

From *The Rainbow Fish*:
deep   blue   sparkling   proud   silent

Adjectives the children may suggest:

| gold | spotted | slippery | boogly-eyed | breathing |
| fast-swimming | gray | brown | blue |

Create a cumulative poem (four or five lines) by adding a new adjective on each line. You may want to vary the pattern on the last line. Discuss how changing the pattern at the end adds interest.

Gold fish
Gold, *slippery* fish
Gold, slippery, *gray* fish
Gold, slippery, gray, *spotted* fish
Gold, slippery, gray, spotted, *boogly-eyed* fish
And all very blue fish.

Now let children write their own cumulative poems. Afterward, sitting in a circle, have them read their poems and tell something they have learned about poems—for example, the "mind pictures" the words create.

➤ Day by day, introduce new concepts related to description:

■ Listen to and read poems.
■ Observe and describe pictures.
■ Bring in objects—leaves, toys, a fancy hat—to feel and describe.
■ List verbs.
■ List adjectives.
■ Play "close your eyes, turn your back, name something you remember seeing, add a descriptive word."
■ Bring in a box of shapes to write cumulative poems about; a tree, a triangle, a bear. Let children make additional shapes.
■ Play a game matching descriptive words to an animal: big– whale, small–mouse.
■ Play "think of an animal, now add a word to describe it."

➤ As a way to make children more responsible for their learning and allow for children's varied rates of progression, list the poems that are assigned each day on a flipchart or the board. Children can check this list to see how many they've done.

Experienced writers will complete the assigned poems and accompanying drawings more quickly than their classmates. Let them choose to write additional repetitive or cumulative patterns. Direct their attention to lists of verbs and adjectives to use in their poems.

Rhyme

Don't assume that the children know what rhyming is. Young children in particular may have a fairly vague perception of rhyming, thinking, for example, that *shop* rhymes with *tap*. Have children listen to the last part of rhyming words (the rime), not the beginning parts (the onset).

➥ Before children write rhyming poems, they should listen to and read nursery rhymes and other rhyming chants and songs. During shared reading you could cover up a rhyming word (or part of a rhyming word) and ask the children to predict what it will be or substitute alternative rhyming words.

➻ Mention that words may sound the same but be represented by letters that look different. Write rhyming pairs of words on cards in large print and hang them around the room at a height the children will be able to reach and read with a pointer.

➻ Prepare some "rhyme packages" (with the rhyme written on a sheet with blank spaces and the missing rhyming words written on separate cards) for the children to manipulate and read.

Hickory, Dickory, __ __ __ __ | dare |

The pig flew up in the __ __ __ | air |

The man in __ __ __ __ __ | brown |

Soon brought him __ __ __ __ | down |

Hickory, Dickory, dare.

➻ Play a game in which the children clap every time they hear a rhyming word.

➻ Reinforce the concept that rhyming words have the same sound by playing a game with musical instruments. Bring in two each of several kinds of instruments—two drums, two kazoos, two triangles, and so on. Tip two tables or desks on their side and have a child hide behind each one with a set of the instruments and alternate playing the instruments (sometimes the same one the other child has just played, sometimes not). Have the rest of the children in the class say if they sound the same or do not sound the same.

➻ Play a circle game in which one child states a word and the next child gives a rhyming word.

Writing Poems with AA Rhymes

➻ Choose short, four-line rhymes on which to make innovations. Some children may find it easier to work in paired groups, but others may want to work independently.

➽ Read the poem "It's Raining, It's Pouring":

It's raining, it's pouring
The old man is snoring
He went to bed
And hit his head
And couldn't get up in the morning!

Prepare sheets of paper containing parts of the poem:

It's _____ it's _____
The _____
She _____
And _____
And _____

During shared writing, come up with ideas for similar lines and rhyming words as in "It's Raining, It's Pouring." Then have children independently compose similar rhyming poems. They can add illustrations and bind the sheets together into a book.

➽ Have children write "Look in the . . ." poems using the same initial repetitive pattern and placing rhyming words at the end of lines:

Look in the canoe to find the __ __ __ __ __ __ | paddle |

Look on the horse to find the __ __ __ __ __ __ | saddle |

Look in the flower to find the __ __ __ | bee |

Look in the forest to find the __ __ __ __ | tree |

Read "Fred Told Me" and have the children create their own innovations:

Fred told me he saw a frog
In the kennel, with the dog

_____ told me, he/she saw a _____
(child's name)
In the _____ with the _____

Provide other short rhymes each day for the children to innovate on.

27

Poetry

One, two	One, two
Buckle my shoe	_____
Three, four	Three, four
Shut the door	_____
Five, six	Five, six
Pick up sticks	_____
Seven, eight	Seven, eight
Shut the gate	_____

See the candle shining bright	See the _____
We will light one every night.	We will _____

Elephants walk like this and that	_____ (animal)
They're terribly big and terribly fat	They're _____
They have no fingers and they have no toes	They _____
But goodness gracious what a nose.	But _____

Do you think a fish might like	Do you think _____
A ride on a bike	A _____
Do you think he might care	Do you think _____
To sit on a chair?	To _____

Other poems with the AA rhyming pattern that you can innovate on are "Twinkle, Twinkle, Little Star" and "Incy Wincy Spider."

➥ In a box, put a number of three- or four-letter word cards that easily rhyme with other words. Have children draw two or three words from the box and use a word at a time to write a rhyming couplet:

bed	At night I go to bed, Wearing pajamas, bright red.
hop	Hear a rabbit hop, hop, hop, Along the road bop, bop, bop

➥ Have students recite poems. Tell the children and their parents that several children will be reciting a poem in the classroom from memory each week. It may be a poem they have created or a published poem they have been reading. They will be judged on speaking loudly and clearly, remembering the lines, and using appropriate expression.

Send the following card home to let parents know that their children are doing this week's poetry talk. They may want to help them prepare their recitation.

I am doing a poetry talk this week on _____.

I have chosen to

☐ Recite an entire rhyme or poem

☐ Talk about my drawing of a poem and recite some lines

☐ Storytell my poem and recite some lines

© 2005 by Liz Simon from *Write as an Expert*. Portsmouth, NH: Heinemann.

Limericks: The AABBA Rhyme Scheme

A limerick is a humorous or nonsense verse that has five lines. Lines one, two, and five rhyme, and lines three and four rhyme, in the pattern AABBA. Lines one, two, and five generally have nine syllables each, and lines three and four have not more than six syllables each. (*There Was a Big Fish*, by Janeen Brian and Gwen Pascoe [1992], contains lots of limericks.)

➡ Write some limericks on chart paper in big print with several of the rhyming words missing. (You may want to insert the onset as a scaffold.)

A gardener living in Leeds

Once swallowed a packet of s _____.   seeds

Now the tip of his nose

Is covered with r _____.   rose

And his ears sprout carrots and w _____.   weeds

➡ Write the first two lines of a limerick and have the children complete the rest using the appropriate rhyming and syllable patterns:

Now, a problem occurred at our zoo
When a baby was born to the gnu
— — — — —
— — — — —
— — — — — —

➤ When children write their own limericks, they can begin each with
"There once was a . . ." or "There was a. . . ." Provide support with a
list of humorous ideas: characters from nursery rhymes, funny or silly
actions. Before the children write their limericks, suggest they draw a humorous image and/or write down their thoughts. Remember to publish a
big-book version for the class to read. Your students will love it!

Imagery

Certain poetic techniques help create images and moods, either serious
or humorous. Children can imagine different kinds of images relating
to sight, sound, smell, taste, and touch. Feelings and emotions can be
explored using alliteration, onomatopoeia, and simile, usually within a
rhythmic pattern.

Alliteration

Explain that alliteration means the repetition of initial consonant
sounds in consecutive or close-by words (like tongue twisters).

Read *One Wobbly Wheelbarrow,* by Gwen Pascoe (1994b), and see
whether the children can identify the alliteration.

Six slimy snails,
Five faded ferns

Ask the children to select a set of six consecutive numbers between
one and thirteen, and, using the same pattern as the one in *One Wobbly
Wheelbarrow,* write an adjective and a noun beginning with the same
sound as each number.

Acrostic Alliterative Poems

➤ Children enjoy writing acrostic poems in pairs. Have them
choose a topic and a number of words appropriate to the topic. Then

they can write the topic vertically, one letter on a line, and write a horizontal series of words related to the topic that begin with each letter.

Here's an example. Read *Whale Watching*, by Josephine Croser (1996), and select a word from it on which to base an acrostic poem. There are lots of possibilities: *winter, whale, sand, watch, water, wonder, Antarctica, waves, spray, flippers*. Next write a list of nouns, adjectives, verbs, and adverbs beginning with the letters in the word you have chosen. Suppose you chose the word *whale*. The poem might turn out like this:

	Seeing a **Whale**
watery, wave, warrior, wash, walloping, whack	**W**alloping whack
hulking, harmless, hesitating, hiding, hump	**H**ulking hump
athletic, abode, Antarctica, arching, attractive	**A**bode Antarctica
lump, leaping, large, lashing, lingering	**L**eaping lump
electric, elastic, emperor, ecstasy	**E**lastic emperor

A personality poem is another fun example. First, have the children list a number of personality traits, like *elated, heroic, courageous, adventuresome, daring, bold, brave, calm, cool, clearheaded, thoughtful, kindly, gentle, imaginative, confident, clever, wise, capable, excited, delightful*. (They may want to refer to a dictionary.) Then, each child writes his or her partner's name vertically and thinks of words to describe her or him, choosing words beginning with each letter in the partner's name. For example:

Capable, confident

Helpful, happy

Rugged, royal

Innovative, inquiring

Sure, super

Chris!

Onomatopoeia

Onomatopoeia is the use of words whose sound suggests the sense; in children's poetry these are primarily words that imitate animal and environmental sounds. Using onomatopoeia animates the literary experience for the reader, provoking humorous images and subliminally stirring feelings.

➽ Make sounds by banging on drums, scratching or scraping an object, coughing, and so on and have children make up words to name these sounds.

➽ We easily hear the sounds behind the words in *On a Dark and Scary Night,* by Gail Jorgensen (1988). Reading from the poem, make the sounds for a witch's laugh, a ghost's boo, an owl hooting, and so on. Children can use this (or similar models) as a model for writing poems using words that represent sounds.

➽ Read the big book *Trouble in the Ark,* by Gerald Rose (1975). In the story, all the animals are crowded in the ark. It rains and rains and rains. They become very fed up. A fly starts the trouble:

He *buzzed* at mouse
Who *squeaked* at rabbit

➽ Search through other children's stories and find locutions like *Oh! Arrrr! Ow!* and *Ouch!* Introduce your students to exclamations and the punctuation mark that accompanies exclamations.

Simile

A simile likens something to something more vivid: *as black as night,* for example. The word *like* or *as* is used to make the comparison.

➽ Use the big book *Deep in a Rainforest,* by Gwen Pascoe (1994a):

Deep in a rainforest, the world can be . . .
as red as a parrot

Or use the big book *Birds on Stage,* by Saturnino Romay (1994). The second verse begins:

This bird has an egg like a ball

➽ Remember cumulative poems? Read *Hairy Maclary from Donald's Dairy,* by Lynley Dodd (2001).

During shared writing innovate on *Hairy Maclary from Donald's Dairy.* An example is:

> As small as a snail
> Covered in shell
>
> As small as a snail
> Covered in shell
> Like an Inuit's igloo

➤ A fun way to include similes in poems is to have children write progressive (and positive) comparison poems about someone. Give each child a sheet of paper. Ask the children to write a classmate's (or teacher's or story character's) name at the top. Then they pass the sheet to the child sitting to the left. Instruct the children to write a *like* or an *as* sentence comparing the person named at the top of the page to a *fruit.* After writing the sentence, each child again passes the sheet to the child on the left. Instruct the children to write a *like* or an *as* sentence comparing the person to an *animal.* Continue this procedure three more times, having the children compare their subjects to a *piece of furniture, a type of weather, a time of the day.* The result will be something like this:

> Sweet and succulent as a pear
> Happy and hoppy as a rabbit
> Comfortable like a squashy armchair
> Bright and sparkling as a sunny morning
> Sleepy and relaxed like the end of the day.

Paintings and Poetry

Paintings and poetry are very similar. Both create an image built on significant detail; both use devices and forms that arouse emotional responses, thoughts, descriptions, and interpretations.

➤ Study a variety of paintings—landscapes, action scenes, portraits, still lifes, abstracts, the work of a particular painter. Ask the children to observe closely and take notes in language that aligns with the image they are studying.

➡ Broaden children's perceptions of paintings and poems by inviting an artist or a poet to sit with the children and recount the history of her paintings or poems and what her creations mean to her.

➡ Invite your students to consider different viewpoints: their own as observers and the painter's as the creator. If persons are depicted in the painting, have children imagine what they could be thinking or saying to each other. An abstract painting can engender language that relates to color, shapes, and lines.

➡ Remind children of the possible poetic approaches and techniques they can use as they shape poems based on paintings. Make a class anthology of these poems and include the paintings that stimulated the language and the emotion.

Assessment: Learning Outcomes Profile

After you have taught one or more of these forms of poetry, assess the children's ability to apply what they have learned. Give them at least fifteen minutes to write a poem in one of the forms they have studied. Ask them to read their work and check that their poem makes sense, begins with a capital letter, and ends with an appropriate punctuation mark. Can they add adjectives to make their poems more interesting?

Assess each child's writing by examining it in connection with the achievements listed on the Poetry Learning Outcomes Profile (BLM 1, page 34) and entering either a check mark or an explanation on the form. For example:

> Write a simple poem   √
> Reread poems   *sometimes*

You can also write general comments about the child's overall performance.

POETRY LEARNING OUTCOMES PROFILE
for parents and other teachers

Name _____

Has been studying poetry and is now able to:

Text

Recite a simple poem _____

Write a simple poem _____

Write a complicated poem _____

Match topic and content _____

Contextual Understanding

Make suggestions during class writing _____

Reread poems _____

Text and Language Structures

Innovate on another poem _____

Use a pattern: repetitive phrases and/or
      cumulative verse _____

Present original ideas _____

Provide a title _____

Use adjectives and verbs _____

Use rhyme, alliteration, onomatopoeia, simile _____

Conventions

Use the initial capital _____

Use the final period _____

Use commas _____

Use exclamation marks _____

Additional Comments

_____

_____

_____

_____

_____

CHAPTER 2

Letter

The function of social letter writing is to record feelings or observations, to make requests, and/or to explore or maintain relationships.

Children's social letter writing is like writing about personal experiences (see page 45). The difference is that letters have a particular structure: they are set out in a certain way; there are certain formalities at the beginning and at the end of a letter.

A letter is datelined and addressed to a recipient (when, where, who). The preamble in a letter also considers the recipient: "How are you now after your bout of flu?" The writer can then go on to relate information (what) and sign off (the closing).

There are a number of preparatory activities that you can use as a stimulating lead-in to letter writing:

- Have children make a large mailbox out of a cardboard box and paint it red. Also make a carrier's hat and bag and collect different-colored paper and envelopes.
- Send a note home to parents asking them to handwrite a letter to their child or compose one on a word processor (show how you want the letter set up).
- Construct a huge envelope and address it to the class; write an appropriate large letter from a giant to the class and put it in the envelope.
- Make a chart listing the days of the week and the months of the year.

Figure 6

Letter Program Plan		
Social letters (transitional writers)		
Content		
Social communication and interaction		
Text Structures	**Language Structures**	**Conventions**
Left-hand page orientation Date	Letter tone: personal verses impersonal	Capitals, initial and embedded Periods
Addressee	Awareness of tenses	Question marks Quotation marks
Body of letter: giving information	Varied sentences: asking questions, making comments	Exclamation points
Sign-off on a new line	Descriptive language	
	Reading and writing common words: *how, you, love, write, soon, yours, truly, regards* Proper nouns: months, days	

Activities at the Point of Writing

Learn the days of the week and the months of the year

Make stamps using the computer program Kid Pix® (click on "Goodies," then "Pick a stamp set")

Innovate on *The Jolly Postman* (Ahlberg and Ahlberg 1990): publish a big book and include the letters the children write; place the letters in envelopes glued to the appropriate pages; Share-write the beginnings of letters to the characters in *The Jolly Postman*

Continue share-writing letters to the Jolly Postman and other characters

Make drawings of classmates and label them—personal features, interests, etc.

With the class, create a "Somebody I Would Like to Write To" list: other classes at the school or at other schools, the principal, teachers, family, friends

Identify favorite characters and authors

Visit your local post office (have children write thank-you letters to the post office staff afterward)

Write the days of the week on a medium-size board while the
children observe.

➡ Discuss how to fix the spelling of days and months into memory
by using a Spelling Question Map:

What does it begin with and end with?

Clap out the syllables.

Are there any sound or letter clusters like *ay* and *th?*

Look for small words within words: *Sun, Sat, day*

What are the tricky parts?

➡ Display charts containing the names of the days of the week and
the months of the year for children to read.

➡ Play a circle game in which children read the names of the days
and the months, which have been printed on cards (other words can be
added later). Designate one child as the mail carrier and give him a hat
and a mailbag. The other children sit in a circle chanting:

Here comes the mail carrier,
Ha ha ha!
Who will get a letter today?

The mail carrier hands a card (*Monday,* for example) to someone,
and if he or she reads it correctly, the card is placed in the mailbox.
Remind a child who cannot read the word about strategies he uses. Tell
if necessary.

➡ Read stories involving the days of the week, like *The Very Hungry Caterpillar,* by Eric Carle (1975).

➡ Read *The Jolly Postman, or, Other People's Letters,* by Janet
and Allan Ahlberg (1990). Children love to take the various types of
correspondence out of the envelopes and read them.

Beginning a Letter

➼ Model beginning a letter to the Jolly Postman, stressing the setup.

> Tuesday, May 10
>
> Jolly Postman
> Home
>
> Dear Postman,
>
> How are you after your long trip around the countryside?

On future days, have children begin letters to the other characters in *The Jolly Postman:* the Three Bears, the Gingerbread Man, Jack, Cinderella, the Wolf, Goldilocks. Model again as necessary.

➼ Have the children spend time looking at and sharing letters they have brought from home.

➼ As necessary, hold conferences with individual children about how to begin a letter.

Body of the Letter and Sign-Off

➼ Model writing the body of a letter to the Jolly Postman. Ask children for ideas, spelling, and punctuation. Connect information that lets the reader know what the writer looks like and what interests her or him with the following art activity: have the children, in pairs, make drawings of each other underneath which they state the person's eye color, hair color, age, games he or she likes to play, names of brothers, sisters, pets, favorite TV show, and so on.

Make the children aware that in a letter, they can tell about their experiences, ask questions, and tell funny stories or jokes to make the reader laugh. Stress the use of descriptive words to make the letter interesting.

At the appropriate time, add the sign-off.

➼ Use *The Jolly Postman* as a model for a big book in which to publish the children's letters. It could begin:

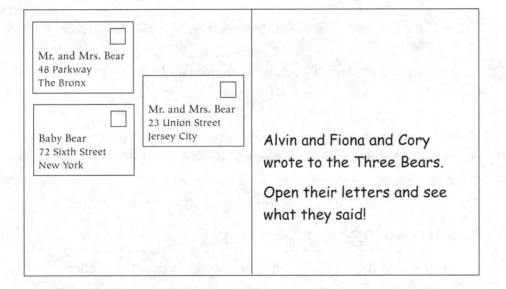

Once upon a motorcycle,

So they say,

Class 204 wrote letters

to Nursery Rhyme characters!

Mr. and Mrs. Bear
48 Parkway
The Bronx

Baby Bear
72 Sixth Street
New York

Mr. and Mrs. Bear
23 Union Street
Jersey City

Alvin and Fiona and Cory wrote to the Three Bears.

Open their letters and see what they said!

Making Envelopes

➥ Have the children unfold an ordinary envelope to see how it is constructed. Once they have the hang of it, they can make their own envelopes for the letters they write. (Note: Use commercial envelopes for assessment purposes; you will be assessing only whether they can address an envelope, not their skill at making one.)

Writing Letters for a Purpose

➥ Have children complete their letters to the Jolly Postman characters.

➠ Read the class the letter from the giant that you prepared. As a class, write a reply to the giant's letter.

➠ Children write a reply to their parents' letters.

➠ Arrange for the children to write letters to children in another class.

➠ Point out that emails are a kind of letter.

➠ Read "The Three Billy Goats Gruff" (Galdone 1973) and have the children dramatize it. Then ask them to write letters to the class next door relating the story, how it was acted out, the characters' feelings, and the consequences of the characters' actions.

➠ Have children write to another teacher, who will then reply.

➠ After the post office visit, write thank-you letters to the workers involved.

➠ Have the children write to whomever they'd like to. (They may choose a person from the "Somebody I Would Like to Write To" list.)

Proofreading

➠ Children should be encouraged as soon as possible to correct their own work. Tell them to be sure to reread every letter they write. Show children how they can proofread their letters using the Letter Proofreading Guide (see BLM 2, page 42). Enlarge a copy of this guide and display it in the classroom so children can refer to it when they are proofreading their letters.

Assessment: Learning Outcomes Profile

To assess the children's letter-writing skills and knowledge, give them a sheet of paper on which to write a letter and an envelope to address. Allow thirty minutes for writing and ten minutes for proofreading. Ask them to refer to the Letter Proofreading Guide.

Assess each child's writing by examining it in connection with the achievements listed on the Letter Learning Outcomes Profile (see BLM 3, page 43) and entering either a check mark or an explanation on the form. For example:

Write a simple letter   √
Use new lines for setout items   *very well done*
   (e.g., date, addressee)

You can also write general comments about the child's overall performance.

LETTER PROOFREADING GUIDE

I can proofread my letter by asking these questions:

Have I started with the date?

Have I addressed it?

Have I given an opening greeting?

Have I given an ending?

Have I used new lines when I had to?

Does it make sense?

Have I used capital letters where I had to?

Have I used periods where I had to?

LETTER LEARNING OUTCOMES PROFILE
for parents and other teachers

Name _____

Has been studying letter writing and is now able to:

Text

Write a simple letter _____

Write a more developed letter _____

Contextual Understanding

Make suggestions during class writing _____

Proofread his/her work _____

Text and Language Structures

Organize the text: _____

    Date _____

    Addressee _____

    Greeting _____

    Body _____

    Closing and sign-off _____

Use new lines for setout items (e.g., date, addressee) _____

Address the envelope _____

Conventions

Use the initial capital _____

Use the final period _____

Additional Comments

_____

_____

_____

_____

Notes

Recounting

The function of recounting is "tell[ing] events for the purpose of entertaining or informing. Events are usually arranged in temporal sequence" (DSP Literacy Project 1988). Recountings include personal observations, past experiences, and published stories.

This is a very comfortable genre for children. Early writers relate personal experiences and simply and sequentially recount stories that have been read to them or that they have shared when reading big books. Transitional writers' understanding about stories is developed through inquiry and text deconstruction: they learn how authors create ideas and structure stories to engage readers' attention. They explore literature and develop knowledge and skills to confidently take the next step to becoming authors themselves.

Lead-In

➥ Relate recounting to real-life experiences: point out that current-events and history programs on TV are oral (spoken) recountings. Written recountings include biographies, autobiographies, and diaries and journals.

Personal Experiences

➥ Begin with children's own experiences. Introduce the practice of telling their experiences orally or, if they are already doing this, make it more formal. Give the children a Personal Experiences Plan containing the key

Figure 7

Recounting Program Plan

Personal experiences (early and transitional writers)
Stories (transitional writers)

Content

Personal experiences (early writers: "I went"; transitional writers: a particular experience, narration)
Imaginative stories (inquiry: How do authors make stories?)

Text Structures	Language Structures	Conventions
Title Content matches title	The maintenance of the past tense	Initial capital letter Final period Embedded period and subsequent capital letter
There is an orientation: a setting, a time, and a place (transitional writers describe settings)	Adjectives, verbs, adverbs	
Characters are introduced (transitional writers describe appearances and feelings and explore roles and relationships)	Pronouns	Other punctuation as appropriate
Events and ideas are sequenced Problem–solution	Text cohesion: Time-sequence adjectives and adverbs: *first next, later, after, finally* Conjunctions: *and, also, or, then, after that, just, then, soon, meanwhile, so, but*	Separate paragraphs: setting, event(s), ending
Ending resolves the problem Comments and opinions (optional) Reasons (include examples from the text) Recounting Proofreading Guide		

Activities at the Point of Writing

Prepare personal experiences plan: Where? When? Who? What? How did it end?

Present verbal retellings: personal news; stories; a walk where you stop, look, and listen (any interesting animals along the way?)

Read big books, picture books, fairy tales, novels

Play Numbered Heads in groups of four (see page 47)

Use sets of sequencing pictures (Schaffer 1988; boxed three- or four-picture sequencing cards) to put the events of a story in order

Create story maps, story webs, flap books (with flaps that open like windows to reveal drawings or writing)

Role-play a character

Model how to retell a story orally, in drawings, and in writing

Prepare recounting plans

List describing words from texts

words *where, when, who, what,* and *how* (see BLM 4, page 48). Have them use this plan sheet to draw or write the main ideas of their personal experiences.

The *mood* of a personal experience recounting is informal; it is told or written in the first person. Early writers generally tell an everyday experience: *I went to the shop with Mom. Mom bought me a pair of shoes.*

A personal experience can be a particular event, something important or funny that happened, a memorable holiday experience, or the first visit to the dentist, hairdresser, or doctor, for example.

➥ As your writers mature, model more descriptive writing during shared writing. Sound like a narrator, getting the audience to feel and experience your observations. For example, use language like *I remember when; if you only knew how I felt; you may have had the same experience.* Include dialogue: *I said, "You may not think that." He replied, "I don't think so."*

➥ Read Roald Dahl's *The Magic Finger* (1998) as a model of language a narrator uses: "I can't stand . . . ." "Before I was able to stop myself. . . ."

Story Inquiry

➥ Help children begin the process of understanding how authors create ideas and structure stories and language to engage the reader's attention by asking, *How do authors make stories?*

➥ Read lots of big books and picture books, and allow time for children to explore them, note ideas, and ask questions. Use their questions to create a chart on what goes into making stories:

What do authors write about?
What language do they use to convey the meaning?
Why is the story funny?
Do the illustrations extend the story?
Why is the setting in a forest? Could the setting be somewhere else?
Could the story ending be different?

➥ Read picture books and, with the question *How do authors make stories?* in mind, play Numbered Heads. Have children sit in

PERSONAL EXPERIENCES PLAN

BLM 4

Draw or write about something that has happened to you.

Setting

      Where?

      When?

Who?

What happened?

How did it end?

circles of four, and give each child in a group a number: one, two, three, or four. Read a part of the text, then stop and ask a question like *How did the author begin the story?* or *Who is the main character?* Let group members put their heads together and quickly discuss the answer. (Children with poor concentration or immature learning development will be encouraged by their peers to remember the answer.) Then ask specific-numbered persons in each group to answer the question.

What was the title?
Who was the author?
Where and when did the story happen?
What happened first?
Who was the main character?
What do you think the main character was like?
How do you think the story will end?

Story Structure

➥ Read fairy tales and use sequenced pictures (see Frank Schaffer's *Fairy Tale Sequencing* [1988], for example) to show that stories have a logical order or a pattern. The awareness of patterns in writing enables children to build concepts and visualize the structures, language, and ideas in stories. After you have read a fairy tale, have the children work in pairs: one retells the story while the other partner sequences the pictures.

➥ Repeatedly read big books, placing the following cards next to the appropriate places in the text:

➥ Orally retelling the main events of the story is another way to help children internalize story structure. Make children aware of the traditional construction of stories: the orientation, the plot, a problem and a solution, the sequencing of events, the main characters and their roles within the story. Encourage children to begin their oral retellings by repeating the opening lines of the published text ("One dark night," for example).

Display a chart to help children remember what to include in their retellings:

> The title is _____
>
> The author is _____
>
> It happened _____
>
> The main character is _____
>
> The story began like this:
>
> _____
>
> Next, _____
>
> Then, _____
>
> After, _____
>
> Finally, _____

➦ Give transitional writers a sheet with jigsaw shapes (see BLM 42, page 172). After you or the children read a story, ask them to write the story ideas sequentially in the pieces of the jigsaw. Students cut out the jigsaw and read and reassemble the pieces. (This is a great partner activity.)

➦ After discussing the happenings, characters, and settings of a particular text, ask pairs of children to write as many ideas about the story as they can on strips of paper. Then have them sequence the ideas and eliminate those that they think are minor. Ask them to glue the remaining ideas in order on a sheet of paper.

➦ *Story maps* or *story webs* (also called *graphic organizers, concept maps,* or *mind maps*) can help children learn about story structure. After you or the children read a story, they could use the computer programs Kidspiration® (kindergarten through grade 5) or Inspiration (grade 6 through adult) to map the main ideas of the story. (These programs include many different shapes that match settings, plot elements, and characters; for example, if the story is set in a house, children can map the ideas using house shapes.)

Characters and Settings

➻ Use *role playing* to let children interpret and explore characters' reactions, feelings, and traits. Role playing helps children move out of themselves and think and act as the character in the story: they can write about the story as if they were that character. When role playing Sid in *Six-Dinner Sid,* by Inga Moore (1997), for example, they can describe his feelings and experiences as he goes from house to house eating six dinners a day, having six names and personalities, sleeping in six different beds, being scratched in six different places, and to top it off, taking six doses of medicine!

➻ View the illustrations in picture books. Often it is the illustration, not the words, that tells you about a character's feelings and reactions. Often it is the illustrator who determines the setting. Let the children examine and describe the pictures in books and discover the unwritten nuances.

Recounting Repetitive Stories

➻ Read *Five Little Monkeys Jumping on the Bed* (Christelow 1991) and compare ways of recounting information. First retell the story word for word:

> Five little monkeys were in the bed and one fell out.
> Four little monkeys were in the bed and one fell out.
> Three little monkeys were in the bed and one fell out.

. . . and so on through to one monkey. Then model how to eliminate irrelevant detail and write only the important aspects. Show them how they can recount this story without duplicating the repetitive parts:

> Five little monkeys were in a bed. One at a time they fell out until there were no monkeys left in the bed.

Endings

➻ How did the author end the story? As you read a variety of books, list the different endings of stories. Innovate on some endings by changing some of the words or the idea.

➨ Critically analyze some endings. For example, *Cinderella* and *Alex and the Glass Slipper,* by Amanda Graham (1991; both stories are contained in one book), have a "lived happily ever after" ending. Ask children's opinions about the endings of these two stories and their reasons for accepting or criticizing the endings, and solicit their suggestions for different endings.

Recounting in Writing

➨ Children can begin recounting their personal experiences or stories by drawing what has happened. Illustrations help children visualize settings, character reactions and feelings, and the unfolding of the plot. Then they can use their drawings to write their recountings.

➨ Have children recount imaginative stories by making books with lift-up flaps that reveal parts of the story (see BLM 5, page 55). The recounting is organized under the flap headings *When, Where, Characters, Story Middle (1st, 2nd, 3rd, 4th),* and *Story Ending.* Children cut along the dotted lines indicated on the template and paste a blank sheet of paper behind it, being careful not to glue down the flaps. Then they write the appropriate information under each flap. They can recount the story by opening up the flaps in sequence.

➨ Read a different story each day and have children recount it using a flap book, a Story Map (BLM 6, page 57), or, a graphic organizer (BLM 43, page 173).

➨ Model using the Recounting Proofreading Guide (see BLM 7, page 58) to encourage children to edit and correct their work. After each writing session, have children refer to an enlarged and displayed version of this guide and circle spellings they perceive as incorrect, add punctuation, and make sure the story makes sense.

➨ During the writing sessions, hold conferences with a manageable number of children each day to see how well they understand structures and language features. Have criteria in mind:

- How secure is the children's use of tenses and verbs?
- Are they using adjectives? Put small colored dots on places in the child's work where he or she could add an adjective.

■ Are they using the traditional story structure?

■ Are they linking ideas using sequencing terms? Put small colored dots on places in the child's work where he or she could add a sequencing term.

➼ Model how more confident writers can at times form small groups and, using one criterion at a time, honestly and sensitively assess one another's work. It's important for children to learn from each other. It also gives you the opportunity to individually help writers who are having problems.

Language Structures

Adjectives

Although adjectives should not be overused, including some adjectives helps provide "mind pictures" of features and characteristics. When children use adjectives, they expand their statements and ideas, making their recountings more creative and interesting.

Text Cohesion

➼ Encourage children to link their ideas using words or phrases like *the next day, later on, first, finally.* Read books that have examples of these sequential links. For example, in her story *Clarence and the Great Surprise,* Jean Ekman (2001) sequences events using phrases such as *after a few minutes, that evening, the next morning,* and *after breakfast.* Creating compound sentences using conjunctions (*and, but, as, because*) and adverbs (*suddenly, quietly, loudly*) also helps link ideas.

Assessment: Learning Outcomes Profile

When you feel that your students' recounting skills have developed to a suitable point (after approximately five weeks), choose a story and read it to the children twice, without discussion. After the reading, have them spend thirty minutes writing their recounting of the story, five minutes writing their opinion of the story, including justification, and another five or ten minutes proofreading using the Recounting Proofreading Guide (BLM 7, page 58).

Assess each child's writing by examining it in connection with the achievements listed on the Recounting Learning Outcomes Profile (BLM 8, page 59) and entering either a check mark or an explanation on the form. For example:

Write a developed recounting	√
State an opinion about the story and give a reason for that opinion that relates to the text	√ *did so in an amusing way*

You can also write general comments about the child's overall performance.

BLM 5

1. Cut the flaps open on the dotted lines.

2. Paste around the edge of a blank sheet and attach to this page.

3. Lift the flaps and draw or write.

where

characters

Story beginning
Title
Author

when

(Continued on following page)

BLM 5 (continued)

2nd

4th

1st

3rd

Story middle

Story ending

STORY MAP

By drawing or in writing, recount the story you have read.

Name: _____   Date: _____

Title: _____   Author: _____

_____

Characters:

Beginning:

Middle:

Ending:

RECOUNTING PROOFREADING GUIDE

I can proofread my recounting by asking myself these questions:

Have I got the title?

Have I got *where* (described where the story takes place)?

       when (told when the story takes place)?

       characters (described the main characters)?

       happenings (introduced a problem)?

       ending (presented a resolution)?

Have I kept to the same story?

Is it in order?

Does it make sense?

Did I start with a capital letter?

Did I finish with a period?

Did I use a period at the end of each sentence and begin the next sentence with a capital letter?

Did I use other punctuation? (? ! , " ")

Have I checked my spelling and circled unsure spellings?

RECOUNTING LEARNING OUTCOMES PROFILE
for parents and other teachers

Name _____

Has been learning about recounting and is now able to:

Text
Write a simple recounting _____
Write a developed recounting _____
Match topic and content _____
Sustain a topic _____

Contextual Understanding
Make suggestions in class _____
Reread his/her own story _____
Proofread and make corrections _____

Text and Language Structures
State the title _____
State the author _____
Use story structure: _____
   Describe the setting: where, when _____
   Describe the character(s): who _____
   Sequence the events _____
   Use language to link time: *first, then, later, finally* _____
   Provide an ending _____
State an opinion about a story and give a reason
  for that opinion that relates to the text _____
Maintain the correct tense _____
Use adjectives to enhance the recounting _____

Conventions
Use the initial capital letter _____
Use the embedded period and the subsequent capital letter _____
Use the final period _____
Use other punctuation: ? ! , " " _____
Recognize incorrect spelling _____
Use some paragraphing _____

Additional Comments

_____

_____

Notes

CHAPTER 4

Fiction

The function of fictional narratives is to explore the imagined experiences that other people have. They are primarily entertaining, sometimes informative.

What children have understood from recounting stories is reinforced and referred to constantly during the fiction unit. The children are now authors of their own imaginative stories.

During fiction writing, children write adventure stories in which the events happen to real people (e.g., Billy gets lost on a family camping trip) or they write fantasy stories in which the heroes are animals who speak and wear clothes or are imaginary characters such as the beautiful princes and ugly witches portrayed in folktales and fairy tales. The fantasy plot usually involves the simple goodness of a hero overcoming problems caused by a villian, and generally magic and fantasy develop or resolve the plot. Fantasies are generally short stories, and the settings (castles with towers) and the characters (princesses and ogres) set the mood.

There are many language features to explore during the creation of fictional writing. Examining how ideas are expressed in big books, deconstructing and constructing texts in front of children, and reinforcing this learning in literacy centers will help children use adjectives (which describe a noun), adverbs (which tell the how, when, where, or why of a verb), dialogue (and the accompanying quotation marks), and alternative verbs for *said* (*whispered* and *shouted*) for example.

Figure 8

Fiction Program Plan

Adventure (transitional and extending writers)
Fantasy (transitional and extending writers)

Content

Adventure (events that could happen to real people) and fantasy stories (characters are animals, witches, and so on, and magic and fantasy develop or resolve the plot).

How do I write engaging stories?

Text Structures	Language Structures	Conventions
Story beginning	Written in third person or first (dialog)	Initial and embedded capital letters
Setting: where, when (describe the setting)	Verbs: past tense (regular: *-ed*; irregular, *took*)	Periods Other punctuation: ? ! , " "

Characters: who (describe the characters)	Adverbs: *how, when, where, why* of a verb	Paragraphs
		    transitional writers:
		    beginning, middle, end
		    extending writers:
		    all paragraphing

Middle: plot
Initiate events (cause)
	Cohesion of text by using phrases:
	    It began . . .
	    In an instant . . .
	    Without any warning . . .
	    All of a sudden . . .	

Sequenced happenings
    effect, what
    problems
characters face and solve
	Cohesion of text by using time-sequence adjectives and adverbs:
	    first, next, later, after, finally,
	    then, after that, just,	

	Conjunctions: *and, also, but,* *then, soon, meanwhile, so, or*	

Climax (leads to ending)
Ending: resolution
	Vocabulary adds tension:
	    immediately, suddenly, loudly,
	    softly	

Match between title and topic Sustain topic	Adjectives: quality, feeling, quantity, classification	

Story plans	Varied sentences:
	    statements, questions, commands,
	    dialog	

Fiction proofreading guide	Make writing interesting –
	    alliteration, onomatopoeia, similes,
	    and metaphors for extending writers
	    (connect to poetry study)
	Wide range of vocabulary, synonyms	

(Continued on following page)

Figure 8 (*Continued from previous page*)

Activities at the Point of Writing

Ask children to recall what they know about recounting; then ask, *What do you know about writing fiction?*

Read nursery rhymes showing simple traditional story structure: character, problem, solution

Read fiction books and make a "story starters" chart (see page 65)

Model a story from beginning to end; later, make it into a big book and/or dramatize it

In groups, read stories to one another and offer criteria-based constructive criticism

Sit in a circle and tell a story orally (give the children cards: *when, where, who, happenings,* and *ending*)

Tell stories by manipulating pictures and phrases (titles, characters, settings, and so on) on a chart

Revisit stories used in recounting and innovate on them

Add endings to nursery rhymes, fairytales, and folktales

Show wordless texts to stimulate ideas

Read fantasy (e.g., *Charlotte's Web* [White 1974]) and fairy and folktales and compare plan by drawing and labeling

Use Narrative Challenge as an alternate experience (see page 84)

Use the Adjective Classification chart (see page 75)

Make a "Words That Link Ideas" chart (see page 78)

Highlight a fiction characteristic: *Today we are looking for _____ in your writing.*

This framework focuses on traditional narrative, particularly *imaginative* story writing, to include

- *Beginning*: setting (where, when, weather conditions) and introduction of the character(s) (Transitional and extending writers are encouraged to describe the setting and characters.)
- *Middle*: the plot, the cause and effect, the problem, the climax; the events stated sequentially (Extending writers are more aware of the language associated with cause, effect, and climax.)
- *End*: a resolution to the dilemmas that have occurred

Lead-In

➡ Encourage children to make links between recounting and writing fiction. Write these questions on a large sheet of paper:

What do you know about writing fiction?
What do you remember about how authors make stories?
What do you remember about writing a recounting?

Read the question about writing fiction first, then go on immediately to how authors create stories and what the children remember about writing recountings. After the children have given their responses, return to the fiction question and let the children suggest connections. The main idea is this: *before, they were recounting the work of other authors; now, they will become authors in their own right.*

Narrative Structures in Nursery Rhymes

Nursery rhymes are especially great for showing traditional story structures. They have a setting and characters, a simple, fast-moving plot, and a problem, but not always a resolution.

Character	Humpty Dumpty
Setting (cause)	Sat on a wall,
What happened (effect, problem)	Humpty Dumpty had a great fall.
Resolution (which failed and caused another problem)	All the King's horses and all the King's men
	Couldn't put Humpty together again.
Character	Pussy cat, pussy cat
Setting (cause)	Where have you been? I've been to London
What happened (effect, problem)	To visit the queen. . . .
	I frightened a mouse under her chair.
Resolution (not determined)	
Character	Little Boy Blue
Setting	[farm, meadow, haystack]
Cause	Come blow your horn, [because he hasn't blown his horn]
What happened (effect, problem)	The sheep's in the meadow, The cow's in the corn.

Where is the boy
Who looks after the sheep?
He's under the haystack
Fast asleep.

65

Fiction

Resolution (not determined)

Later, when children are studying narrative endings, they can write endings that resolve these indeterminate endings.

Story Beginnings

➥ Have a selection of picture books, big books, and short novels available for the children to read. Have the children, working in small groups of two or three, write down the opening sentences of these books.

➥ Begin a generic "Story Starters Chart" and look for examples of story starters during shared reading. Read through the list of story starters each day.

```
                    Story Starters

    It was . . .

    One morning . . .

    Once there was a _____ who . . .

    Long, long ago . . .

    Once upon a time . . .

    The other day . . .

    There was . . .

    Last night . . .
```

➥ Extending writers can experiment with other story starters:
dialog: "What is happening," said Ali.
an action: Jim slurped his drink.
a feeling: Destiny was becoming impatient.

Writing Fiction Beginnings

➡ During shared writing, create a class story. Model writing the story, using ideas supplied by the children:

Start with a title. Look at the "Story Starter Chart" and choose a beginning. Then move on to the setting and a character. Describe Sam's reaction to the big bang.

> ### The Monster
> Last night, from the middle of the dark forest, Sam heard a BIG BANG. Sam was scared. His hair went completely spiky. . . .

Stop there. *Each day for a week,* model beginning a new story. At the end of the week, put them all to one side. (Later, the children can vote on which story beginning they would like to continue during shared writing. The draft done during shared writing can be published as a big book, and the children can provide the illustrations.)

➡ Each day have the children write a fiction beginning, read it to a partner, and give some constructive criticism on the partner's writing based on this checklist:

Does it have a title?
Did the writer include a setting using adjectives?
Has the author introduced a character?
Is there some description of the character?
Now say something positive about your partner's writing.

Setting and Character Description

Describing story settings (time, place, and the weather conditions) creates a mood, a feeling that gives a hint about what is to follow. The words appeal to the senses—*misty shadows,* for example. Visual representations enable children to fill in more imagined detail.

➡ Have viewing sessions in which children look closely at how the illustrators of picture books have captured or created settings.

Setting Description

The setting is _____

Draw

The place and the weather

Write

A description of your setting

➼ Have children draw a variety of settings: the beach with white, frothy waves; mountains with thunderclouds; and so on.

➼ During shared reading, examine types of characters and how they are portrayed in stories. Generally, the main character is depicted through her or his words, actions, and reactions to what is happening in the story. Sometimes a character's appearance and reactions are interpreted by the illustrator. Characters may have unusual traits, may repeat things over and over again, or have a trait that changes during the story.

➼ Generate a list of *feeling* words that describe characters: *lonely, cowardly, happy, calm, cool, courageous, kindly, gentle, imaginative, confident, sure, excited, capable, wise, confused, delightful, jumpy.*

➼ Ask the children to make detailed drawings of characters. Alternatively, partners can role-play a story and write down what happened (including the dialogue).

➼ As a model, read *The Ugly Duckling* (Johansen 1996) and really bring to the children's attention the setting the duckling moves in, its appearance, and the reactions it has to what is happening. Children

CHARACTER DESCRIPTION

The main character is _____

DRAW

What you think the main character looks like

WRITE

What does the main character do?

What do you think the main character might say?

How do you think the main character feels about what is happening?

can imagine what the duckling would be saying if it could talk. They
can add speech bubbles to their drawings of the duckling or indicate
feelings by the way they draw the eyes or the beak.

Have children tell a story from one of the ugly duckling's siblings'
point of view. They can imagine what the brother or sister duckling
could be thinking and write these thoughts in bubbles.

➼ When children have main characters in mind for their stories,
have them imagine, improvise, and create their own scenarios and use
language to express the reactions and emotions of the characters.

Cumulative Oral Narrative

➼ Telling narratives orally is important in learning to write fiction,
and you should have children begin doing so when you introduce happenings and events. On days when you are not modeling writing the
class story, conduct circular oral storytellings in which each child
builds on the previous storyteller's ideas. Begin this activity as a whole
class; later, children can work in groups of eight.

First, have the children make a set of cards that identify elements of
narrative structure: four *beginning* cards—*title, when, where,* and
who—and four *what* (happening) cards that sequence a series of
events—*what began it, what happened next, what happened after that,*
and *how did it end.*

Title	What began it?
When?	What happened next?
Where?	What happened after that?
Who?	How did it end?

Then have the class sit in a circle, and ask eight children each to
draw a card. These eight children will tell a story, each contributing the
element on the card he or she has drawn.

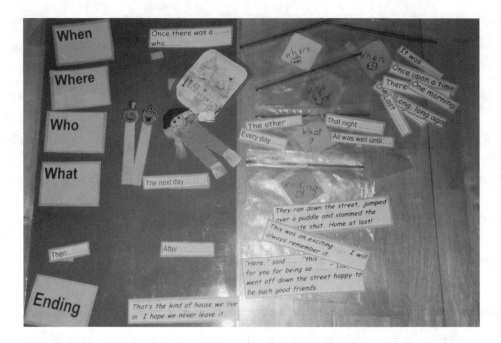

A fair amount of assistance and intervention will probably be required for the first few sessions. To begin you can take each card and model the proper response. You will definitely need to guide children through the plot sequences: the *character* went to *a certain place, said* or *did something* that caused an *effect,* which led to one or more *problems.*

➥ Make a "Tell a Story" chart. On a large sheet of cardboard, place headings and pieces of felt or Velcro®. Cut out pictures of where, who, and events (what), and write when and ending sentences. Put self-adhesive Velcro® spots onto the back of the pictures and sentences. Place the storyboard in a learning center for children to use to guide them through the structure of oral storytelling when they create their own stories.

Story Happenings and Events

The traditional story plot involves an initiating event, a *cause* (for example, *the children were calling loudly in the cave*), followed by sequenced events, the *effects* of the cause (for example, *and all of a sudden they heard a rumble and rocks began to fall and they blocked the entrance of the cave*). From then on, the story deals with the *problems* the characters will face (and ultimately solve) because of what has happened. Finally, the story reaches a *climax* (*All seemed lost. They could not move another muscle, when . . .*).

For extending writers, examining texts, listing phrases relating to cause and climax and mapping a plot (see BLM 9, page 72) assists their understanding and writing about cause, effect, and climax.

Innovations on Established Texts

Let children know that they can innovate on known stories when they write their stories.

➥ Read *The Gingerbread Man* (McCafferty 2002). Maintain the characters of the woman and the fox but change the events. The woman does something different (*cause)*, which produces a different character and reaction (*effect)*, and the new character causes a different *problem* for the woman. The fox solves the problem. The ending (resolution) can also differ from the original text.

➥ Read *Hey, Frog!* by Piet Grobler (2002). Change the characters and setting, introduce a similar problem, and find a solution to the problem. Perhaps a goat eats everything too quickly and hiccups so loudly he keeps the farm animals awake all night. Children will love solving this problem (maybe a nocturnal animal takes the goat out with him on his nightly prowl).

➥ Read *Old Man's Mitten*, retold by Yvonne Pollock (1995), and retain the same beginning (*Once there was*) and the same main character (*an old man who*), but change the plot and the ending.

Ending: The Resolution of the Problem

Endings in fiction writing are difficult for children (they can be difficult for adults too!). They like to put "The End" just as their story is about to develop. Lots of oral and written practice with creating endings is beneficial.

➥ Tell children first to ask themselves who will solve the problem: The main character? Another character? Some outside source (the weather changes, for example)?

MAPPING A PLOT

BLM 9

CLIMAX

EFFECT

EFFECT

EFFECT

CAUSE

➼ Alter the oral storytelling procedure just a little. Have a child sum up the *happenings* in the story so far. Then let everyone discuss different ways of solving the problem(s).

➼ Write new endings for nursery rhymes. You could begin with "Humpty Dumpty":

All the King's horses and all the King's men couldn't put Humpty together again.

But that night a wise old chicken was walking along the road and saw the smashed-up Humpty. "Oh, Humpty, how did this happen? Wait a while and I will get something I use on my broken eggs to mend your shell."

Back came the chicken with a bottle of glue. The chicken sat all night putting all the cracked jigsaw pieces together, and by morning Humpty was rebuilt.

The chicken warned Humpty to never sit on the wall again!

What happened after the mouse was frightened under the queen's chair? What happened when Little Boy Blue woke up? Were the cows and sheep still there?

➼ Write summaries of known stories and ask children to write an ending to solve the problem. (BLM 10, page 76.)

Story Plans

➼ Introduce children to the idea of using a plan based on drawings and labels to envision their stories. Encourage them to make detailed drawings about a story they will write. Tell them to include as many episodes as possible. This type of planning enables children to tell or write much longer and more complex stories.

The plan in BLM 11 (page 77) has space for pictures down one side of the page; the beginning and ending pictures are provided, and the children add the middle pictures. (You could also provide the middle pictures and have the children add the beginning and ending pictures.) Have the children first draw the missing pictures and then write the accompanying story. (If you like, you can have them draw the pictures one day and write the text the next.)

Create sheets with one or two pictures on them (see BLMs 12 and 13, pages 81 and 82). These visual stimuli really help improve the writing output of young writers.

Picture plans assist children's visualization of stories. Eventually, though, children should use a written story plan (BLM 14, page 83) or a graphic organizer (BLM 43, page 173) to reinforce the structure of narrative writing. (They can refer to them when they write their assessment stories.)

➥ Occasionally use a Narrative Challenge to enliven planning and writing. Give children, working in pairs, a chart with the headings *Character, Goal of Character, Problem,* and *Resolution* (BLM 15, page 84). Let them share ideas and ask them to write nine planning possibilities (they can choose characters and events from stories they know). A filled-in planning chart might look something like this (only the top four rows are shown):

Character	Goal of Character	Problem	Resolution
Lizard	To bask in the sun	Kingfisher bites off his tail	Basks where the kingfisher can't fly
Three bears	To go for a walk	Henry breaks into their house	Send Henry an invitation to come on a certain day
Witch	To become a kind character	Witches are bad	Starts doing good deeds
Tiger	To stop being messy	Is always messy	Tries to do different things to clean up but becomes messier

After a pair has entered nine possibilities for each column, tell them to use the final four digits of one of their telephone numbers (let's say 4231) to select a random combination of possibilities from the chart: character–4, goal–2, problem–3, and resolution–1.

Character	Goal of Character	Problem	Resolution
Tiger	To go for a walk	Witches are bad	Basks where the kingfisher can't fly

Then ask each pair to write a (humorous!) narrative following this plan.

Language Structures

Adjectives

➡ Explain that adjectives can be classified into those describing a *quality*, a *feeling*, a *quantity*, or a *classification*. On cards, write adjectives from books you and the children are reading in the classroom and have children place the adjectives under the proper headings on an "Adjective Classification" chart. Laminate the chart and word cards and place them in a learning center for the children to use to classify adjectives independently.

Adjective Classification
Adjectives describe nouns.
There are different kinds of adjectives.

Quality	Feeling	Quantity	Classification
black	furious	one, two, five	collie (dog)
large	sad	few, many	science (lesson)
strong	happy		
stronger			
strongest			

➡ Read big books and picture books that have examples of adjectives.

THE LION AND THE MOUSE

Once upon a time, a mouse got too close to a lion. The lion wanted to eat the mouse. "Spare me," said the mouse, "and someday I will help you." The lion let the mouse go, although he couldn't think of a way a tiny mouse could help him.

One day the lion was caught in a hunter's net. He roared in misery.

Write a new ending:

_____

_____

_____

_____

_____

_____

_____

_____

_____

_____

STORY PLAN WITH PICTURES

BLM 11

Draw the missing parts of the story. Write four paragraphs, each with a new idea.

Text Cohesion

Cohesion is maintained by linking happenings using language that indicates cause, sequencing of events, climax, and solution:

Cause	[In an instant . . . Without any warning . . . All of a sudden . . .] *It began* when Jenny went for a walk with her mischievous dog and she took him off his lead.
Effect	The dog chased a cat up a tall tree.
Problem	The cat meowed and wailed. Jenny tried all sorts of ways to get the cat out of the tree.
Events	*First she . . .*
	Then she . . .
	Next she . . .
Climax	*After a while* Jenny sat down dejectedly. The cat wailed louder than before. It would fall unless she did something.
Solution	*From out of nowhere* a woman appeared with a bowl of cat food. *Immediately*, the cat scrambled down the tree.

Make a "Words That Link Ideas" chart *(adjectives, adverbs, conjunctions)* and find examples in big books during shared reading.

Words That Link Ideas

first	also
then	but
after	suddenly
next	before
finally	immediately
because	later
soon	earlier
and	

Helbertia the Vile, by Yvonne Winer (1990), has wonderful examples of phrases that connect ideas:

At midday	In the cool evening	Now
Early in the morning	By midday	By lunchtime
At last	In the meantime	When at last
Right then	As the sun set	

Assessment: Learning Outcomes Profile

To give you and the children a good view of what they are achieving in their writing, display the following (or a similar) chart. Have children pin their names in the appropriate sections when they have incorporated that particular characteristic into their narrative writing.

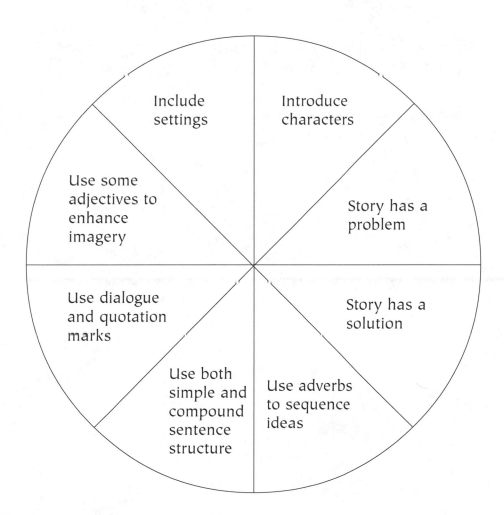

At the end of your fiction study, assess the children over a three-day period (extending writers may need less time). On day one, let them plan their story for fifteen minutes. On day two, have them write from their plan for at least thirty minutes. On day three, ask them to proofread their story using the Fiction Proofreading Guide (which you have enlarged and displayed; see BLM 16, page 85); make any neccessary meaning, language, and punctuation changes; and circle spellings they are not sure about and consult a dictionary for the correct spellings.

Assess each child's writing by examining it in connection with the achievements listed on the Fiction Learning Outcomes Profile (BLM 17, page 86) and entering either a check mark or an explanation on the form. For example:

Write a traditionally structured story   √
Sustain the topic   *mostly*

You can also write general comments about the child's overall performance.

BLM 12

Draw what you think will happen next.

Write about the cat.

VISUAL STIMULI STORY PLAN

BLM 13

Look at the pictures and write a story.

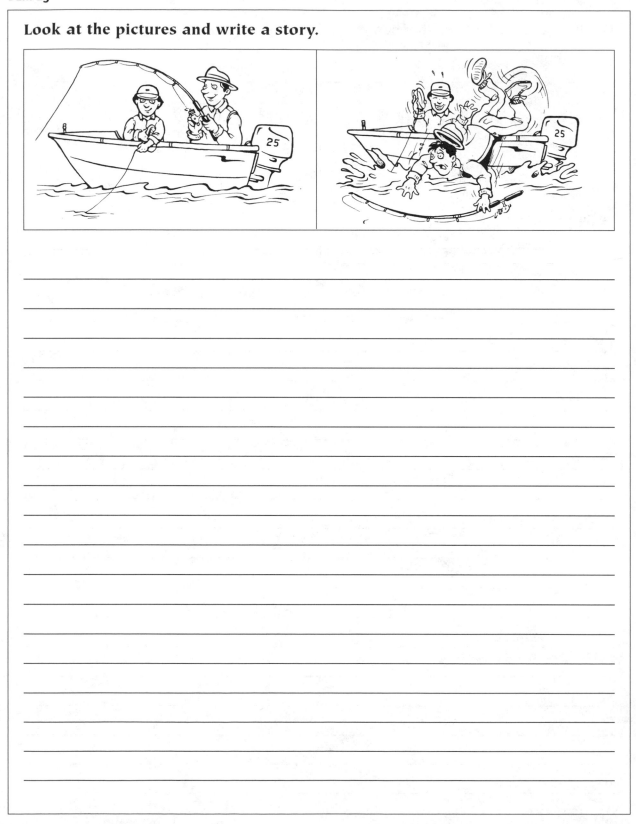

_____

_____

_____

_____

_____

_____

_____

_____

_____

_____

_____

_____

_____

_____

_____

_____

_____

_____

_____

_____

PICTURELESS STORY PLAN

BLM 14

Title	

Setting
   when
 	
   weather
 	
   where	

Characters	

Happenings
   (It began when)
 	
   Then,
 	
   Next,
 	
   After	

Ending Finally,	

NARRATIVE CHALLENGE

BLM 15

1. Write nine planning possibilities for each column. You can use stories that you have read or make up your own possibilities.

2. Use the final four digits of one of your telephone numbers to select a random combination of possibilities for your plan.

3. Write your story using the plan.

	Character	Goal of Character	Problem	Resolution
1.				
2.				
3.				
4.				
5.				
6.				
7.				
8.				
9.				

FICTION PROOFREADING GUIDE

BLM 16

I can proofread my narrative fiction by asking myself these questions:

Have I got a title?

Have I got   *where* (described where the story takes place)?

when (told when the story takes place)?

characters (described the main characters)?

happenings (introduced a problem)?

ending (presented a resolution)?

Have I kept to the same story?

Is it in order?

Does it make sense?

Did I start with a capital letter?

Did I finish with a period?

Did I use a period at the end of each sentence and
begin the next sentence with a capital letter?

Did I use other punctuation? (? ! , " ")

Have I checked my spelling and circled unsure spellings?

FICTION LEARNING OUTCOMES PROFILE
for parents and other teachers

Name _____

Has been studying narrative fiction and is now able to:

Text

Write a simple story _____

Write a traditionally structured story _____

Write an engaging story _____

Match topic and content _____

Sequence ideas _____

Sustain the topic _____

Contextual Understanding

Make suggestions in class _____

Choose a topic _____

Proofread work _____

Make corrections _____

Text and Language Structures

Provide a title _____

State where and when _____

Describe the setting _____

Introduce a character _____

Identify characters by description _____

State happening(s) and develop happening(s) _____

State an ending to solve the problem _____

Use descriptive language (adjectives, adverbs)_____

Use appropriate tenses _____

Conventions

Use the initial capital letter _____

Use the embedded period and subsequent capital letter_____

Use the final period _____

Experiment with punctuation: ? ! , " " _____

Use punctuation: ? ! , " " _____

Use paragraphing _____

Additional Comments

_____

_____

CHAPTER 5

Response

The function of response is to review the qualities of a text, construct critical interpretations, and share those ideas and feelings.

Writing responses and reviews is a genre that children are constantly exposed to. Early writers may draw a picture of the "best part" of a story (judgment) and give reasons for their opinions. Figure 9 shows a second grader's response to *George and Martha 'Round and 'Round* (Marshall 1988):

Figure 9

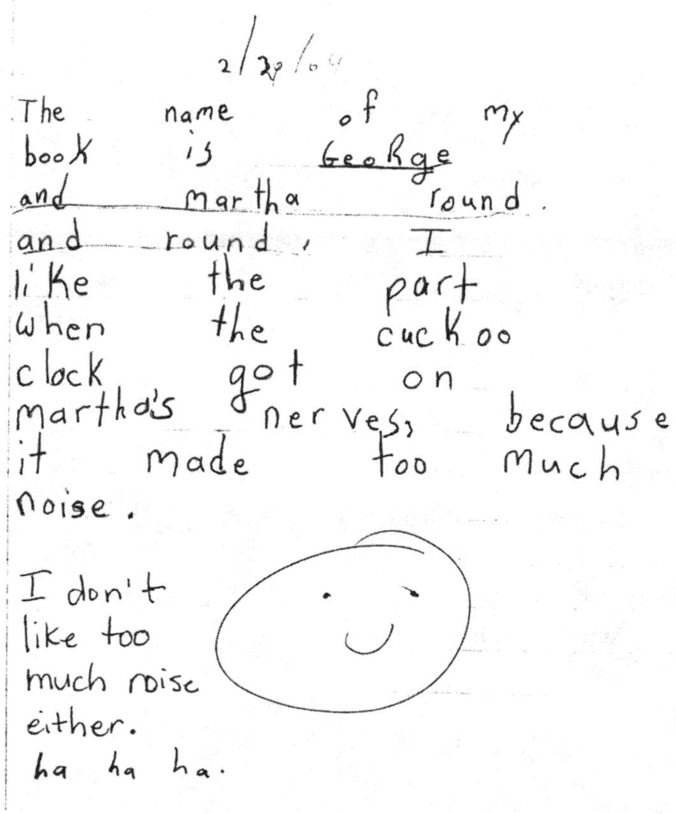

2/28/04

The name of my book is George and martha round and round. I like the part when the cuckoo clock got on martha's nerves, because it made too much noise.

I don't like too much noise either. ha ha ha.

Figure 10

Response Program Plan		
Responses and reviews (transitional and extending writers) *Reading logs, discussion groups, literature circles* (extending writers)		
Content		
Written responses and reviews Reading logs, journals, and literature circles		
Text Structures	**Language Structures**	**Conventions**
Introduction: background information about the work	Author, title, genre, theme	All punctuation Paragraphing transitional writers: introduction, exploring quality, judgment extending writers: all paragraphing
The work's qualities: different texts lend themselves to different explorations (plot, characterization, setting, author's craft, theme, illustrations)	Verbs, noun groups	
Judgment of and recommendation about the work	Value judgments Questions, statements Persuasive language (*You should read this book.*)	
Activities at the Point of Writing		
Read books appropriate for reviewing Examine reviews from newspapers Hold informal discussions about qualities that stand out and provide examples from text Assume roles in literature circles (this requires multiple copies of texts)		

As children develop and mature, their written responses to fiction and nonfiction become more formal.

Training in how to respond to literature includes participating in literature circle discussions and writing notes in reading logs as a way to clarify thinking. This helps move children toward writing independent and interpretive responses to the texts they read.

Lead-In

➻ Ask the children to visualize the various scenarios and the effects of the events on the main characters as you read *Jumanji*, written and illustrated by Chris Van Allsburg (1981). In the story Judy and Peter find a board game in the park and take it home, hoping to alleviate their boredom. And do they ever! The jungle adventure game comes to life. A roaring lion sits on a piano, monkeys steal food from the kitchen, and monsoon rains pour down inside the house. A guide is lost, they encounter a stamping rhinoceros, a python wraps itself around the mantel clock, and a volcano erupts from the fireplace. At last they reach Jumanji, the golden city, and the game ends. Everything goes back to normal. Judy and Peter are exhausted. But is the game truly over? Judy and Peter look out the window and see two boys running through the park with a long thin box. The reader is left with the expectation that these children will have the same exciting but exhausting experiences Judy and Peter had.

Response Format

➻ Clip a "Background Information" card to the side of a piece of chart paper.

Using shared writing, create a paragraph that names the author, the illustrator, the genre, and the theme (what is important to the author).

Background Information	*Jumanji*, written and illustrated by Chris Van Allsburg, is a story full of exciting adventures experienced by Judy and Peter, the main characters, as they play the jungle adventure game. This is Chris Van Allsburg's second book; his favorite theme is mixing fantasy with reality.

Next, read *Jumanji* again and have children explore the *qualities of the text* in discussion groups. Ask each group to choose a quality that really stands out for them: the plot, the setting, the characterization, the author's craft, the theme, or the illustrations. (Different books will emphasize different qualities.) It is important to model a conversational approach for participating in discussion groups. Begin with a comment, an opinion (*I think*), followed by a generic question (*What do you think?*).

Ask the groups to back up their opinions by stating why they chose the quality they did and giving examples from the text. For some children the contrasting settings make this text stand out: *We chose the setting, because in the ordinary house extraordinary things happen. Peter and Judy find an amazing game in the park. As they play the game their house turns into a jungle. . . .* Other groups may choose the plot, because it is complicated or fast-moving or includes a recurring detail. Still others may choose the author's craft because of the language or the unusual ending, which suggests that new characters may have the same experiences.

After the discussion, continue to share-write the response.

Qualities of the Work	The contrasting settings really added to the excitement of the story. Can you imagine a lion on a piano, monkeys destroying the kitchen, a large snake on the mantelpiece?
	I felt as though I were experiencing the game; I could feel how Judy and Peter felt. At first they thought they had found an ordinary game in the park. But as the game progressed, they became frightened and worn out. . . .

Finish share-writing the response and review by making a *judgment* and a *recommendation* about the story.

Judgment/ Recommendation	The plot moved quickly and I could hardly wait to turn the page to see what would happen next. You should read this story.

Children can also respond to nonfiction text as the class in the photograph above is doing. The qualities that children would look for in nonfiction texts relate to how the information is presented, whether the information is easy or difficult to understand, whether the information extends knowledge about topic, and how the author deals with the technical language of the topic. A further quality is the organizational characteristics of the text, for example, headings, labels, diagrams, layout of the print and images, the glossary, and index.

Exploring Text Qualities in a Reading Log

As they read, children should write about the text in a reading log. This log will help them be fully prepared when they come together in discussion groups to share views and discuss aspects of the books they have read.

As they share their points of view, they will find that their thinking is clear and that they are able to state their interpretation, evaluation, and analysis of the text in a way everyone understands.

By examining reading logs, teachers can appraise their students' interpretive and analytical thinking.

Literature Circles

For students to be able to write freely in reading logs, they must be carefully trained to respond in the best possible way. A good way to do that is to introduce literature circles (Daniels 1994), which involve independent reading and cooperative learning. Students choose their books and manage their own grouping and discussion. [Each member of a group (no more than five) needs a copy of the book the group has chosen.]

➡ So that students will be able to carry out productive discussions, start out by giving each group a copy of the Literature Circle Role Descriptions (BLM 18, page 95) and each student a Literature Circle Role Sheet (BLM 19, page 96) as models for their behavior. (Enlarge and display the Literature Circle Role Descriptions so children can refer to them when writing "your job is to.") The roles, which rotate with each new book, allow students to internalize the requirements of lively, text-centered discussions.

The *discussion driver* prepares some *open-ended questions* to stimulate the discussion and keep it going. Initially, you may need to make all the children in the group discussion drivers and model how to make comments and ask questions that will stimulate discussion: *I found this part interesting [funny, sad]; what do you think? I thought the main character was such-and-so; what do you think?* In addition, on the discussion driver's role sheet you could state how many questions (most likely beginning with the key phrases *why might, how could,* and *what if*) the driver needs to ask. Eventually, you will want the discussion driver to have in mind questions about the qualities (theme, plot, characterization, setting) that stand out in the particular book being discussed.

As they become more adept at asking open-ended questions, you initially assign other roles to each student. Keep a chart so students can, later, organize their role taking.

The *connector* finds *relationships between the text and real life between the text and other texts.* On the connector's role sheet you could state: *How does the story or character relate to real people? Similar events? Other books? Other writings by the same author?*

The *passage picker* chooses *parts of the story* that he or she thinks are worthy to be read aloud to the group (in other words, special examples of the author's craft): colloquial phrases; language that creates sympathy, antipathy, mood, emotion; passages that affect readers' perceptions, show a change in character, create suspense, and so on. On the passage picker's role sheet, you could state: *Choose a funny or scary or interesting or descriptive part. Write down the number of the page on which the passage appears and tell why you chose it.*

The *word wizard* looks for *special words* that are new and different or important to the text. On the word wizard's role sheet you could state: *Choose words that are new, different, strange, funny, interesting, important, or hard. State the word, the number of the page on which it appears, and why you chose the word—how it fits into the story, what it means (if you know).* The word wizard can bring dictionaries to the group discussion or have ready the meaning of the word.

The *artful artist* either draws a picture of an aspect of the story (character, setting, exciting incident, climax) or points out illustrations in the book that complement or extend the story. On the artful artist's role sheet you could state: *Choose a character, the setting, a problem, an exciting incident, a surprise, or a prediction of what will happen next. Draw it on the role sheet or on a larger sheet of paper. You can also point out illustrations in the book and explain why they are particularly effective.*

The eventual aim is for students to write open-ended logs and converse freely about books they have read. Once students are familiar with literature circle procedures and are able to carry them out smoothly and effectively, they can abandon the role descriptions and role sheets and discuss pieces of literature extemporaneously, marking the pages they want to refer to with sticky notes or bookmarks.

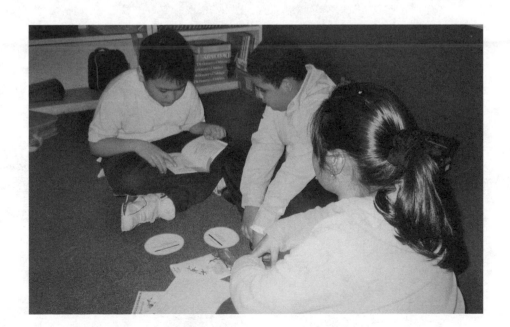

Assessment: Learning Outcomes Profile

After studying the response genre, read a story two times. After the second reading and without referring to the texts students can note some key words and phrases to refer to when they write a review of the story.

Assess each child's writing by examining it in connection with the achievements listed on the Response Learning Outcomes Profile (BLM 20, page 97) and entering either a check mark or an explanation on the form. For example:

> Write a response that introduces   √
>   a piece of writing
> Give background information   √ *very well done*

You can also write general comments about the student's overall participation in discussion groups and the quality of his or her journal entries.

LITERATURE CIRCLE ROLE DESCRIPTIONS

LITERATURE CIRCLE

DISCUSSION DRIVER

Your task is to write some open-ended questions to stimulate the discussion.

You have to keep the discussion going.

You have to get everyone to contribute.

LITERATURE CIRCLE

PASSAGE PICKER

Your task is to choose parts of the story that you think are worthy to read aloud to the group.

LITERATURE CIRCLE

WORD WIZARD

Your task is to look for special words: new words, different words, words important to the text. If you don't know what the words mean, look them up in the dictionary and write down the meanings.

LITERATURE CIRCLE

ARTFUL ARTIST

Your task is to draw something about the story (a character, the setting, an exciting part) or point out illustrations that complement or extend the story.

LITERATURE CIRCLE

CONNECTOR

Your task is to find relationships between the text and real life and between the text and other texts you've read or heard.

LITERATURE CIRCLE ROLE SHEET

BLM 19

Role
Name **Book title** **Group members**
Your job is to:

Look at the role descriptions. Write your role in the top box. Write the description of your role in the box underneath "Your job is to."

RESPONSE LEARNING OUTCOMES PROFILE
for parents and other teachers

BLM 20

Name _____

Has been studying response writing and is now able to:

Text

Write a general response _____

Write a response that introduces a piece of writing,

explores qualities present in it, and offers an opinion of it _____

Match topic and content _____

Sequence ideas _____

Contextual Understanding

Understand that different books lend themselves

to different qualities _____

Make suggestions in class and in small groups _____

Proofread work _____

Improve writing _____

Text and Language Structures

State the title, author _____

Give background information (e.g., author, theme) _____

Choose a quality to emphasize _____

Provide information about the quality _____

Use descriptive language (adjectives, adverbs)_____

Use appropriate tenses _____

Use a mixture of simple and compound sentences _____

Conventions

Use the initial capital letter _____

Use the embedded period and subsequent capital letter_____

Use the final period _____

Experiment with punctuation: ? ! , " " _____

Use punctuation: ? ! , " " _____

Additional Comments

_____

_____

© 2005 by Liz Simon from *Write as an Expert*. Portsmouth, NH: Heinemann.

Notes

Report

The function of a report is to present factual information about something.

In this genre framework, transitional writers learn to plan and write a descriptive report on the basis of key words. The report begins with a statement introducing the subject—a classification or generalization. Early writers describe a few features of animals (e.g., A penguin swims in water.) This introduction is followed by descriptions of the animal's characteristics. Children need to have plenty of prior information to draw on when they begin to write their reports.

Showing children how to read for information will be most important during the study of this genre. You may need to extract information from texts and rewrite it at different levels so all children can read the material independently. Color code the difficulty levels, and let the children choose their favorite animal. (Some publishers have a line of leveled nonfiction, such as Rigby's PM Library Animal Facts books.)

In this genre framework, extending writers write inquiry-based reports on varying topics. They first explore existing reports to determine the appropriate structure: content, organization, language, and vocabulary. Then you determine a significant, open-ended, nonjudgmental question (*Are rain forests important?* for example) to investigate. Before beginning their research, the students have a shared experience (watching a video, reading a big book, or examining pictures about the topic) in order to establish a knowledge base. Then they identify three or four aspects of the topic that puzzle them, ask and prioritize appropriate questions, and carry out systematic research.

Figure 11

Report Program Plan

Informational (animal) report (transitional writers)
Inquiry-based report (extending writers)

Content

Report about animals:

- Reading for information and noting key words
- Introduction (opening statement describing a class of animals)
- Description of features and characteristics

Inquiry-based report on varying topics:

- Topic choice
- Significant, open-ended, nonjudgmental question
- Resources and discussion to formulate questions to investigate
- Relevant information, key words, summaries
- Table of contents, glossary, headings, explanations, labels, diagrams, index, photos, illustrations, tables, graphs

Text Structures	Language Structures	Conventions
Informational report:	Impersonal, factual	Initial capital letter
Title	Nouns: mostly maintain singular or plural throughout	Final period
Introduction: opening sentence stating the class animal in general terms		Embedded period and subsequent capital letter
	Descriptive detail (verbs, adjectives, adverbs)	
	Third-person pronouns *(it, she, he, they)*	Other punctuation: ! , " " ?
Sequenced information	Mostly present tense (exception: past tense if extinct)	
Characteristics: habits, habitat, appearance	Modifiers: *all, every some, many*	Paragraphing: introduction, each characteristic
Headings and key words	Text Cohesion	
	Simple and compound sentences	
	Conjunctions: *and, because, as, but, or*	
	Technical terms: *mammal, amphibian, bird, reptile, diet*	

Inquiry-based report:

Questions to lead research

Organizational/graphic elements (table of contents, graphs, headings, maps, diagrams, photos)

Key words/summaries

 (Continued on following page)

(Continued from pervious page)

Activities at the Point of Writing

Informational report:

Build knowledge about particular animals

Go to a zoo

Plan classification activities: what questions should I ask? (see BLM 21, page 104)

Find the differences and similarities between animals

Read big books and informational books about animals

Show examples of how reports are written

Play What Is It? with cards or books (see page 109)

Play word bingo using technical words [Make bingo cards with six words on each one, in separate squares. A "caller" reads the words and players place a marker on the word called. The first to cover the six words on the board wins the game "Bingo."]

Show pictures and have the children describe the animal

Model writing a report, beginning with the introduction and using key words to plan a descriptive report

Choose headings (characteristics) and put sentences in order under them (group work)

Note key words

Work with a partner and individually to construct report

Use planning sheets and graphic organizers (e.g., Kidspiration® computer program)

Explore resources: ask questions and note results

Inquiry-based report:

Ask and prioritize questions

Note key words and/or summarize

Use the Internet: search the Web and investigate specific sites

In gathering material for the report, children develop a number of research skills:

- Listing predictions about the topic
- Asking questions about problematic issues
- Searching for appropriate material
- Selecting relevant information, taking notes, and summarizing
- Using key words as planning devices

Lead-In: Informational (Animal) Report

➤ Most reports begin with a general classification of the animal being discussed. Help children become familiar with animals' classifications based on their characteristics. Collect lots of pictures of animals from books and magazines and place them in envelopes. Then make a chart like the one below:

Mammals	Amphibians	Reptiles	Birds

Have children work in groups of four. Give each group an envelope of animal pictures and ask them to classify the animals under the headings on the chart. Have them use the Classification Question Guide (BLM 21, page 104), which you should enlarge and display.

Report Introduction

➡ Establish that the report should begin with a general statement of the animal's classification. Have the children practice this:

A tiger is a mammal.

Headings, Key Words, and Sequencing

➡ Read a big book about elephants (or some other animal of your choosing) to the class, and ask children to come up with four general headings they could use to plan a report on elephants. For example: *Classification* (What type are they?), *Appearance* (What do they look like?), *Habitat* (Where do they live?), and *Habits* (How do they move? How do they breed? What do they eat?). Divide a large sheet of paper into four sections, one for each heading.

Tell the children that in order to plan their report they will need to note key words. Then, prompted by these key words, they will be able to write the report in their own words.

Read the big book about elephants again and model finding the key (main) words to write under the headings. If children are familiar with the terms, explain that key words are generally nouns, adjectives, verbs, and adverbs. For example:

Classification	Appearance	Habitat	Habits
largest land-living mammal	powerful trunk ivory tusks (teeth)	Africa (larger) India (smaller) vegetation water	peaceable slow-moving

Then have the children use these key words to create sentences, first orally, then in writing. Ask pairs of students to write a report about elephants:

> The elephant is the largest land-living mammal. The African elephant is larger than the Indian elephant. An elephant lives where vegetation and water are plentiful. It is a peaceable and slow-moving animal. The elephant has a powerful trunk and ivory tusks, which are really teeth.

➡ Have children practice identifying key words. Read a sentence while the children just listen. Then read the sentence again and ask children to write down the key words. Begin by reading general sentences only. Ask the children to isolate two or three key words. For example:

> The *car* is red.
> The *summer* is very, very *hot* and *humid*.

CLASSIFICATION QUESTION GUIDE

BLM 21

To classify an animal, ask yourself these questions:

Does it feed its young?

Does it lay eggs?

Does it have a pouch?

Does it have wings?

Does it have feathers?

Does it live on the land and in the water?

Does its body go hot in the sun and cold in the shade?

➼ Once children are fairly secure in their ability to identify key words, read aloud some more short texts about animals. Let children indicate the key words, and have a fairly confident writer model writing the key words under the headings *Classification, Appearance, Habitat,* and *Habits.* (Any inappropriate words can be discussed and eliminated later.) After each demonstration, ask children to use the listed key words to create spoken or written sentences.

➼ Have children use a Report Plan (BLM 22, page 106) to record key words when they are researching an animal for their report. (*Kidspiration*® is a wonderful computer graphic organizer children can use as well.)

➼ Scramble the title and sentences of a report on a large sheet of paper and have children cut them into strips and reorder them.

They live in the Antarctic, where there is ice and snow and it is very cold.

Emperor penguins are black and white with yellow on their chests.

The male penguin looks after the egg and keeps it warm.

Emperor penguins are birds.

They also eat fish and krill.

Emperor Penguins

Reading for Information

When people read informational text, they intentionally seek to gather relevant ideas and assimilate technical words associated with the topic. Readers look for information that suits their purpose. Children are often dealing with unfamiliar content and vocabulary and the flow of the narrative is interrupted by graphic elements. To assist children:

➼ Deconstruct informational texts during shared reading and show children how nonfiction texts work. For example, isolate parts of texts

REPORT PLAN

Subject: _____

Title of Piece Read: _____

Write key words under the appropriate headings.

Classification	**Habitat**
What are they?	Where do they live?

Habits	**Appearance**
What do they do?	What do they look like?
What do they eat?	
How do they move?	

and explicitly show them how the text and graphic elements, a diagram, labeled pictures or a glossary relate to each other.

Model comprehension strategies:

- How readers ask themselves 'I wonder if . . .' questions, infer (I assume that . . .) and search texts for answers. Headings and key words assist them when finding answers to their questions.
- How children preview the cover, contents page and scan the inside of books for appropriate material to read.
- Get children to close their eyes and visualize a piece of information you read to them.

➥ Children's understanding is enhanced when they turn to a partner and discuss questions asked by the teacher.

➥ When introducing technical or uncommon vocabulary, show children problem-solving strategies such as using a glossary (meaning), searching for small words, and looking closely at tricky parts. Then reinforce this knowledge by involving them in group activities such as bingo games.

➥ Help children whose reading skills are still developing by supporting them through

- Read Aloud
- Partner reading
- Guided reading
- Simpler information. For example, look at these two approaches to similar information:

Bilby

The bilby is a marsupial. It lives in Australia. It looks like a cross between a rabbit and a bandicoot. The bilby is about the same size as a rat. Its fur is a gray-fawn color and it has long ears and a long snout. It has a black band on its tail. The bilby lives in open woodland in the dry parts of Australia. The bilby burrows deep into the ground to make its nest. At night it comes out to hunt for food. It eats insects and grubs and small mammals. In autumn the female has its young, usually two at a time.

Bilby

The bilby is a marsupial. It lives in Australia. It looks like a rabbit and is about the same size as a rat. Its fur is gray. A Bilby has long ears and a long snout. It lives in the woods and burrows deep into the sand. It hunts for food at night. The bilby has one or two young.

➥ Create large books with headings (classification, appearance, habitat, and habits) on each page and sentences of information. Place these books in a literacy center for children to reread and reinforce their knowledge about content and report writing.

Place adhesive Velcro® strips on the cover and each page as well as on the backs of laminated topics and sentences. Ask children to put the appropriate topic on the cover and put the sentences under the appropriate headings and in the appropriate order.

Language Structure

Descriptions

Although a report is fairly concise, it is more interesting when adjectives are used because they help readers form better mental pictures. Comparative adjectives (*big, bigger, biggest*) are often found in factual reports that compare and contrast different types of things.

➤ Reinforce the use of descriptive language by reading *Birds*, a collection of eight books by Debbie Simmonds (1998). Have children make "What Is It?" cards or books describing these birds. Have other children guess what birds are being described.

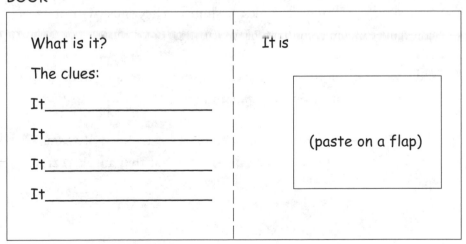

Children could also draw a part of an animal (a webbed foot, for example) and have other children guess what animal that part belongs to.

Singular or Plural

The subject of a report is usually either consistently singular or plural, but sometimes both constructions are used. Point out that plural nouns require plural verbs.

> Snails *live* in most places in the world.
> Snails *have* a very unusual way of eating.
> Most land snails *eat* plants.

And remind children that singular nouns require singular verbs.

> A snail *has* feelers.
> If a snail *is* frightened, it can hide.

Also, point out that nouns and pronouns must be singular or plural as their antecedents are singular or plural:

> snails . . . they
> a snail . . . it

Compound Sentences

Some published texts use simple sentences:

Stars are born in space. They can last for trillions of years.
Astronauts can go outside the shuttle. They must wear a spacesuit to keep safe. (Croser 2000)

Tell children that simple sentences can be joined into a compound sentence by using conjunctions like *and* and *but*:

Stars are born in space, and they can last for trillions of years.
Astronauts can go outside the shuttle, but they must wear a spacesuit to keep safe.

Modifiers

Words like *most* and *some* can be used to generalize information.

Lead-In: Inquiry-Based Report

➡ Ask, *What are reports?* Let students find the answer to this question by

- Discussing in small groups what they remember about informational reports
- Exploring (deconstructing) lots of different reports and discovering:
  - The variety of topics
  - How a topic is introduced (for example, by a generalization)
  - The varied headings (for example, in a report on the Iroquois Indians, headings could be *Past Lifestyle, Hunting,* and *Iroquois Indians Now*)
  - How descriptive language is used
  - How information is organized (for example, table of contents, glossary, headings, explanations, summaries, diagrams, index, graphic elements)
  - How text is made cohesive
- Recording their reflections on and questions about reports (*What is a glossary? Why have indexes?*)

Posing an Inquiry

➡ After you have decided on a topic in conjunction with the class (plants, for example), ask an initial significant, open-ended, nonjudgmental, succinct question related to the topic (*Are plants important?*).

Posing Questions to Direct Investigations

Material about a topic can be understood only if students formulate their own questions and systematically investigate those questions.

➡ Introduce the topic by providing a shared knowledge base: read a text aloud, conduct an Internet search, show a video or film, go on a field trip, examine artifacts.

➦ For approximately a week, set aside time each day for students to explore and discuss a variety of resources. Ask them to note their ideas and the questions they would like answered, either in their journals or on the Exploring Resources Question Sheet (BLM 23, page 116). Their questions related to plants might be

> What is a plant?
> How do plants grow?
> Do plants need humans?
> Why do humans cut down trees?
> Are there laws about plants?
> Are all plants good?

Have students prioritize which questions will be investigated. (They could vote.)

Have students use the questions to develop, gather, and select relevant information. Ask them to note key words and summarize information. (Journals are ideal for recording information and planning reports.)

As students create new understanding, more questions may arise.

Inquiry Journal

➦ Students need to keep track of their work in an inquiry journal. For example, after reading the book *Everglades* (George 1995), in which a Native American storyteller tells five children how the Everglades was formed (shared knowledge) you can display the following inquiry question in big print and have the students copy it into their journals:

Are the Everglades significant?

Students then record in their journal their first impressions of the topic.

> I think there is lots to learn about the Everglades and what is happening in the Everglades. Also, I think it is interesting because there is history to learn.

To begin the research, you may want to show a video that presents information about the history of the area, ecological damage, restoration efforts of the Everglades and have the students draw two columns in their journals and (in pairs) discuss, identify and write down the problems and solutions. (See Figure 12 for an example.)

Also have the students begin to ask and list their own questions in their journals, which they will later research. One student's questions are shown in Figure 13.

Figure 12

Problems	Solutions
People not sensitive to wilderness-cleared land for housing and farming Irrigation-drainage Miami spreading	They are now reclaiming farms— reconstructing Everglades
Pollutants from ~~fam fr~~ farms— scientists believe they cause mutations?	
An invasive plant has caused loss of habitat and is endangering panthers	Digging up that plant— this is stripping the land

Figure 13

My Questions

How big was the Everglades?

Do we need the Everglades?

What is the invasive plant called?

How much land has been stripped of trees?

Will the trees and plants come again?

As students research the topic they may make adjustments to questions they have asked or ask new questions. For example:

It said that the Caloosa tribe who lived in the Everglades 500 years ago lived in harmony with the land. *What does live in harmony mean? Are there other civilizations that lived in harmony with the land? (American Indians? Australian Aborigines?)*

Will the Everglades renew itself?

Inquiry journals not only include questions and research notes but all the work that is associated with the topic. Cross-curriculum studies are also included:

- Creating maps that show where the Everglades is, the size the Everglades was originally and the size it is now, and the surrounding area
- Making time lines that detail when the Spanish and Seminoles came; the settling of Miami, and the growth points of the area
- Doing science research that includes study of the region's plants, animals such as the American alligator, crocodiles, sea turtles, birds, the Florida panther, and manatees; and pollutants, mutations, and whether pollutants dissipate over time
- Writing poems about the Everglades
- Reading biographies and distinguishing fact from fiction; viewing how the people's experiences match information gathered from other resources
- Reading stories and noting questions, opinions, and comments (and later, forming discussion groups)

As children are learning about their topic it is worthwhile to stop every now and then and have them write a "Dear Journal" letter. They can reflect on their progress and recount information they have read, outline how their research is progressing, describe their feelings about the study and write about anything else they may wish to mention.

Draft and Publish

➥ Ask extending writers to refer to their journals and plan and write their reports. They can write out a rough draft by hand or type it using a computer program (Kid Pix®, MicrosoftWord®, or Microsoft Publisher®, for example).

➺ Ask them to proofread their rough drafts (see BLM 24, page 117, which you should enlarge and display) and make corrections.

Possible topics for inquiry-based reports include

Endangered species	The Pilgrims	Polar regions
Rain forests	Zoos	The universe
Iroquois Indians	Seashores	Railways

Significant, open-ended questions that relate to those topics could be

Is surviving on planet Earth easy?

Was the migration of the Pilgrims significant?

Are the Antarctic and the Arctic the same?

Are rain forests important?

Why are people interested in the universe?

How did Iroquois in the past differ from Iroquois now?

Is it important to keep animals amused in a zoo?

Do seashores change?

How important are railways to communities?

Webquest is an Internet site that promotes inquiry-based research.

EXPLORING RESOURCES QUESTION SHEET

BLM 23

Topic _____

Title _____

Essential question(s): _____

_____

As you explore resources, ask questions about things that puzzle you and that you want to find out about.

☐ _____

_____

☐ _____

_____

☐ _____

_____

☐ _____

_____

☐ _____

_____

☐ _____

_____

☐ _____

_____

☐ _____

_____

☐ _____

_____

☐ _____

_____

REPORT PROOFREADING GUIDE

I can proofread my report by asking myself these questions:

Have I stated the title?

Have I stated an introduction?

Have I used my key words and my own words?

Have I put the information in order?

Have my questions been answered?

Did I begin with a capital letter?

Did I put a period at the end of the report?

Did I put a period after the end of an idea and begin the next idea with a capital letter?

Have I used , ? ! " "

Assessment: Learning Outcomes Profile

After you have taught the report genre, assess children's ability to apply what they have learned. Inquiry-based reports are written over a period of time, and assessment will be ongoing. You should observe and take notes about a student's participation in discussion groups and his or her journal entries and final presentation.

Assess each child's writing by examining it in connection with the achievements listed on the Informational Report Learning Outcomes Profile (BLM 25, page 119) and the Inquiry-Based Report Learning Outcomes Profile (BLM 26, page 120) and entering either a check mark or an explanation on the form. For example:

Research and write a report	√
Sequence information	√ *includes all detail*

You can also write general comments about the child's overall performance.

INFORMATIONAL REPORT LEARNING OUTCOMES PROFILE
for parents and other teachers

Name _____

Has been studying how to write reports on animals and is able to:

Text

Write a simple factual report _____

Research and write a report _____

Match topic and content _____

Contextual Understanding

Make suggestions in class _____

Ask questions and investigate _____

Read information _____

Extract key words _____

Use headings _____

Sequence information _____

Engage and inform readers _____

Proofread _____

Make corrections _____

Text and Language Structures

Use impersonal, factual writing _____

State an animal's classification in the introduction _____

Describe the characteristics of an animal (*appearance, habits, habitat*) _____

Use present tense _____

Maintain singular or plural noun, pronoun, and verb forms _____

Use a mixture of simple and compound sentences _____

Link ideas using *as, because, and* _____

Use modifiers like *most, some* _____

Conventions

Use the initial capital letter _____

Use the embedded period and subsequent capital letter_____

Use the final period _____

Use other punctuation: ? ! , " " _____

Use paragraphing _____

Additional Comments

_____

_____

INQUIRY-BASED REPORT LEARNING OUTCOMES PROFILE
for parents and other teachers

Name _____

Has been studying how to write inquiry-based reports and is able to:

Text

Research and write a report _____

Select a topic _____

Maintain topic relating to inquiry question _____

Contextual Understanding

Formulate questions to direct research _____

Select and gather relevant information _____

Note key words and/or summarize _____

Proofread and make corrections _____

Text and Language Structures

Use impersonal, factual writing _____

Write an introduction _____

Sequence information using cohesive language conjunctions _____

Maintain singular and plural nouns, pronouns, and verbs forms _____

Use a mixture of simple and compound sentences _____

Use modifiers like *most, some* _____

Include many aspects of report writing:

- table of contents, index, glossary _____
- headings _____
- explanations _____
- diagrams, photos, illustrations, tables, graphs _____

Conventions

Use correct capitalization _____

Use all relevant punctuation _____

Use paragraphing _____

Additional Comments

_____

_____

_____

_____

CHAPTER 7

Media Report

*The function of a media report is to present news about current
events, politics, sports, and other cultural happenings.*

In this genre framework the writing is inquiry-based: children ask questions and investigate a topic.

A media report is usually preceded by a powerful headline announcing its gist. (*Banner headlines*, presented in very large type across an entire page of newsprint, often sensationalize an aspect of a media report to attract readers or signal exclusivity.) The lead paragraph reveals key information, immediately providing readers with the essential facts. These facts are then elaborated on in the body of the report.

Most media reports consist of one-sentence paragraphs; few paragraphs exceed three sentences. A media report is written in the third person.

Lead-In

➥ Pose three questions for students to discuss:

What are news reports?
How do journalists get readers' attention?
Is it important that facts are correct when reporting news?

Figure 14

Media Report Program Plan

News report (extending writers)

Content

Headline signaling the gist

Banner headlines attracting readers or signaling exclusivity

Lead paragraph of key information: *who, what, when, where, how,* and *why*

Several paragraphs of elaboration

Text Structures	Language Structures	Conventions
Headline		
Lead-in: key points	Indirect speech	All punctuation
Elaboration	Third person	Paragraphing
Proofreading guide	Sensational words and phrasing	
	Adverbial phrases and prepositional phrases	

Activities at the Point of Writing

Examine news reports in daily papers

Use graphic organizers (Kidspiration® and Inspiration® computer programs)

Explore resources—ask questions, note aspects

Use the Internet

With a partner, construct a media report

Publish a newspaper (report about events at the school)

Invite a journalist (newspaper or television) to visit the classroom

Ask open-ended questions and develop follow-up questions

Conduct research with a partner

➻ Get students to imagine that they are the editor of a newspaper. Explain that an editor prepares and approves a journalist's work for publication. In pairs or small groups, have students cut out news items that interest them. Ask them to assess whether the journalist has provided the elements of a good media report.

As an editor you make sure the journalist has captured exactly the **who, what, when, where, how,** and **why** of an event.

The journalist has

- ☐ Written a **headline** that will attract the attention of readers
- ☐ Written a lead paragraph telling **who, what, when, where,** and **why**
- ☐ Written additional sentences and paragraphs providing more details about **who, what, when, where, how,** and if important, **why**
- ☐ Made the report interesting

Literature as News

➻ Choose several short novels or stories that could stimulate the writing of a news item. One example is *Monsieur Armand,* by Judith A. Martin (1998). In the story, Monsieur Armand is very upset about a honking goose outside his shop. Monsieur A. becomes very violent and even tries to capture the goose in order to serve it as food in his restaurant. But the goose gets the better of him, and Monsieur Armand is forced to change his menu to wild gooseberry tart, which is a huge success.

After reading *Monsieur Armand,* use shared writing to compose a news report with the students:

- Headline: *Restaurateur's Headache*
- Lead paragraph telling who, what, when, where, how, and why: *A restaurateur, Monsieur Armand, went berserk after being constantly harassed by a goose from the farmyard next door.*

■ Additional paragraphs providing more details: *The goose ignored Monsieur Armand's protestations, and Monsieur Armand lost control. He threw soup at the goose, attacked the goose with a carving knife, and . . .*

➥ Have students, working in pairs, plan and write a news report based on another similar story. The reports could be displayed on a poster, or the children could present them orally in a videotaped newscast.

➥ Have students research, write, and proofread (enlarge and display BLM 27, page 126) media reports for a class newspaper, including interviews; world, national, and local news items; the results of sports contests; and so on.

Language Structures

Adverbs and Prepositions

➥ Ask students to look for the *when* and *where* of news items. Talk with them about how adverbs are constructed in sentences.

➥ Prepositions are words used before a noun or a pronoun to express its relationship to the rest of the sentence. Examples are *at, to, in, near, past, along*. Ask students to look for prepositional phrases (*on top of, next to, close by*) in the media reports they read. Many adverbial phrases contain prepositions: the bird flew *to the branch below*.

Indirect Speech

➥ In media reports, people's comments are often reported indirectly: *he said he was disappointed about the reactions of the people*. The journalist gives the essence of the speech without repeating the exact words. Ask students to find examples of indirect speech in the news items they read and evaluate.

Assessment: Learning Outcomes Profile

Assess each student's writing by examining it in connection with the
achievements listed on the Media Report Learning Outcomes Profile
(BLM 28, page 127) and entering either a check mark or an explanation on the form. For example:

Write a news item that engages   √ *amusing item on debate*
   and informs readers
Expand information   √

You can also write general comments about the student's overall
performance.

MEDIA REPORT PROOFREADING GUIDE

I can proofread my media report by asking these questions:

Have I written a *headline* that will attract the attention of readers?

Have I written a lead paragraph telling *who, what, when, where, how,* and *why?*

Have I written additional sentences and paragraphs providing more details about *who, what, when, where, how,* and if important, *why?*

Have I written a report that makes sense?

Have I made the report interesting?

Have I used correct sentence structure? (Does it sound right?)

Have I used a variety of nouns, verbs, adjectives, and adverbs?

Have I used indirect speech?

Have I used correct spelling and punctuation?

MEDIA REPORT LEARNING OUTCOMES PROFILE
for parents and other teachers

Name _____

Has been studying how to write media reports and is able to:

Text

Write a news item that engages and informs readers _____

Match topic and content _____

Contextual Understanding

Make suggestions in class and small groups _____

Ask and investigate questions _____

Read information _____

Proofread and make corrections _____

Text and Language Structures

Provide a headline _____

Create a lead paragraph: *who, what, when, where, how, why* _____

Expand information _____

Use descriptive language _____

Use indirect speech _____

Use adverbs and prepositional phrases _____

Proofread the report _____

Conventions

Use appropriate capitalization _____

Use appropriate punctuation _____

Use appropriate paragraphing _____

Additional Comments

_____

_____

_____

_____

_____

Notes

CHAPTER 8

Explanation

The function of explanation is to describe how or why something happens, is done, or works. Steps and stages usually figure prominently. Topics are primarily scientific, technical, or historical.

In this genre framework, children write explanations of mathematics problems in a mathematics learning journal. They

- State a question or problem and their understanding about what it requires
- Explore and investigate the problem
- Record the sequence of steps undertaken to solve it
- State their understanding of the processes and concepts involved

Explaining how they solved a mathematics problem helps children

- Clarify their thinking about the concepts involved
- Think through the problem and the processes necessary to solve it
- Link new information with known information
- Analyze, organize, and manipulate data
- Reconstruct and reflect on the materials and processes used to solve the problem
- Reveal feelings they have about the task
- Record their thinking in a way that makes sense

Figure 15

Explanation Program Plan

Mathematical processes and concepts (transitional and extending writers)

Content

Reconstructing the thinking engaged in solving a problem

Linking new information with known information

Analyzing, organizing, and manipulating data

Text Structures	Language Structures	Conventions
General statement: identifying the problem to be investigated and telling how it will be solved Exploration and investigation of problem Series of processes or steps sequentially recorded: action 1, result 1; action 2, result 2 (can include hypotheses, predictions; may use diagrams, graphs, flowcharts) Concluding summary ■ special features or operations ■ evaluation: was the goal achieved? ■ opinion about the task ■ real-life applications	Technical language Modal verbs expressing possibility: *might, may*	None (Punctuation and capitalization are not particular focuses in mathematics journals.)

Activities at the Point of Writing

Fulfilling specific math roles in groups of four

Solving mathematical problems individually or with a partner

Choosing the proper equipment

Recording solutions using words, illustrations, and graphics

Publishing a big book of explanations of math problems and solutions

Lead-In: Math Circles

Write about your understanding of a particular math concept isn't a helpful direction. If children are to be able to write freely in math journals, they need to be taught how to do so.

➥ Begin by saying to the children that when they explain how a mathematical problem is solved they view it in small sequential steps and they use mathematical language.

Then set up math circles by adapting the roles and procedures used in conducting literature circles (Daniels 1994). Form four-member groups and assign each member a specific role: the driver, the collector, the describer, and the connector (see BLM 29, on page 132; laminate the individual cards and make enough to be able to give one to each student in each particular role).

- The *driver* forms a general statement or question clarifying the object of the investigation and reminds the group to keep working toward this goal. When the activity is completed, the driver writes a summary stating whether the goal was achieved and what the group came to understand.
- The *collector* assembles and itemizes the materials the group will use.
- The *describer* (assisted by the other group members) uses pictures, words, and graphs to recount, in order, the series of steps used to solve the problem.
- The *connector* (assisted by the other group members) shows how the mathematics task applies to real life—how one might use it while shopping, building a house, or sewing, for example—and indicates how the group members felt about the experience.

Being asked to carry out specific roles helps children internalize the structures and requirements of writing mathematics explanations. Rotate the roles with each new problem until each student has served in each role. (The driver, describer, and connector can record information on BLM 30, page 135.)

MATH CIRCLE ROLE CARDS

Driver

Your task is to make sure everyone knows the object of the activity and keeps working toward that goal.

■ Prepare a general statement or question about the problem your group is investigating.

■ Afterward, state whether or not your group achieved the goal and what you came to understand.

Collector

Your task is to collect and list the materials the group decides to use.

Describer

Your task is to describe, in order, the series of steps used to solve the problem. (The other members of the group will assist you.)

Connector

Your task is to write a statement that sums up

■ How the task connects with real-life experiences

■ How the group members felt about the learning experience

Math Journals

➡ Once children are comfortable participating in math circles and have internalized the procedures of writing mathematics explanations, you can dispense with the role cards and have them make open-ended entries in their math journals.

Explain that they need to think through and record all the parts of an explanation:

- The *object* of the investigation (what the problem is, how to go about solving it)
- The *materials* and *processes* used to solve the problem—each step, in order, and the result of each action
- A *summary* connecting the learning with real life and telling how they felt about the experience (Did they solve the problem? Did the problem remind them of something else? What did they learn?).

Children should write their journal entries either while they are working through the problem or immediately afterward. They can use pictures, words, and graphs. Figure 16 (see page 134) is an example of a child's math journal entry.

➡ Alternatively, they could record their findings using the Math Journal Guidelines Sheet (BLM 30, page 135), which contains an outline students can refer to in order to stay on task, or on a graphic organizer (see BLM 43, page 173). The computer programs Inspiration® and Kidspiration® are also helpful for making graphic organizers. BLM 31 on page 136 contains questions to help students organize their thinking; enlarge a copy and display it in the classroom for students to refer to.

➡ Let groups and individuals choose which explanations they would like to include in a class book titled *Solving Math Problems*.

We skip counted with a calculator. We had to see if ~~catcu~~ we could find some ~~par~~ patterns. First we counted by 5. First we pressed the ~~AC~~ button and then the number 5. We pressed + 2 times Then ~~th~~ we pressed 0 and then ========= lots of times. We wrote down on our slates the numbers we ~~saw~~ saw. 5, 10, 15, 20, 25, 30 35. We saw there was a pattern in the ones. 5, 0, 5, 0, 5, 0, 50 and there was a pattern in the tens 1, 1, 2, 2, ~~3~~, 3, 3 Then we did it agian with a 6. We had 6, 12, 18, 24, 30 At first we thought there wasn't a pattern but when Ali pressed the = some more, 36, 42, 48, 54, 60, 66 we saw that there was a ~~pattern~~ pattern in the ones 6, 2, 8, 4, 0, 6, 2, 8, 4, 0. Wow! We want to do this with some other numbers. We learnt that there are lots of patterns when we count.

MATH JOURNAL GUIDELINES SHEET

BLM 30

Mathematics topic: _____ Date: _____ **Teacher Comments**

Draw   Write

The problem was:

What I/we did:
Action 1

Result

Action 2

Result

Action 3

Result

Did it work? Why? What did I/we learn?
Did it remind me/us of something else?

What would I/we do next time?
Are there questions I/we want to ask?

MATH EXPLANATION QUESTIONS

BLM 31

What is the object of the task?

What materials do I use?

What might happen if I . . . ?

How can I record what is happening?

What have I found out?

1.

2.

3.

What was the important discovery today?

How does the discovery relate to real life?

How do I feel about this math problem?

Assessment: Learning Outcomes Profile

Read students' mathematics journals and evaluate how they approached each problem. In conferences, direct them toward more suitable processes to use, clear up any doubts or confusions, and raise their level of awareness.

Initially, children's mathematical explanations may be spare and rudimentary. But as they become more experienced at solving problems and see how writing about it helps them think through the process, their observations will become more thoughtful and analytical.

Assess each student's writing by examining it in connection with the achievements listed on the Explanation Learning Outcomes Profile (BLM 32, page 138) and entering either a check mark or an explanation on the form. For example:

Clearly observe and explain what he/she has seen	√
Clearly express his/her understanding	√ *always*

You can also write general comments about the student's overall performance.

EXPLANATION LEARNING OUTCOMES PROFILE
for parents and other teachers

Name _____

Has been studying how to write an explanation and is now able to:

Text

Set a goal for an investigation _____

Clearly observe and explain what he/she has seen _____

Conceptual Understanding

Analyze concepts _____

Ask questions about a problem or concept _____

Link ideas _____

Text and Language Structures

Record the problem _____

Record steps and processes without additional comment_____

Record steps and processes along with additional comment _____

Clearly express his/her understanding _____

Use mathematical language _____

Set next learning goal_____

Additional Comments

_____

_____

_____

_____

_____

_____

_____

_____

CHAPTER 9

Persuasion

The function of persuasion is to put forward a point of view that will convince readers to think or act in a certain way.

This chapter and Chapter 10 (on argument and counterargument) are both subgenres of exposition. Both are based on inquiry, which is directed by questions and research. The text and language structures are similar. The difference is that persuasion maintains the same point of view throughout, while argument and counterargument presents reasons both for and against a point of view.

Persuasion sets out to convince readers that an opinion or argument is justified. Both writer and reader are often led to question assumptions under-lying things long taken for granted. It is a more formal form of writing that nurtures exploration, encourages students to state their views, and helps them judge the reliability of their opinions. Inquiry and expository writing broaden students' knowledge and understanding, foster critical thinking, and (because of the research involved) discourage uninformed generalizations.

In expository writing, students state definite opinions and systemati-cally show evidence to support those opinions. The process is illustrated in the diagram on page 143.

Students need to examine many and varied examples of exposition that demonstrate the different ways in which writers state their opinions, explain, criticize, praise, and persuade as they argue a case. Be on the look-out for issues-based literature, like *Lester and Clyde* (Reece 1976), a story illustrating the effects of pollution on natural habitats, and *Viewpoints on Waste* (Martin 1993), a nonfiction work that examines the issue of waste from various perspectives (see Chapter 10).

Figure 17

Persuasive Exposition Program Plan		
Advertisement (transitional writers) *Letter to the editor* (extending writers) *Article* (extending+ writers)		
Content		
Advertisement, letter to the editor, article Single point of view stated in a way that seeks to persuade or change the reader's opinion or attitude Contemporary issues Topic researched (inquiry), main issues isolated, definite position taken Evidence and information to support one point of view Recommendations		
Text Structures	**Language Structures**	**Conventions**
One persuasive point of view Headline or title to capture interest Concise orientation so readers can predict what the piece is about Sequenced argument: orientation (focus) followed by justification (evidence, information) Concluding statement summing up and making a recommendation	Technical words Mostly impersonal voice Emotive language Mixture of simple, compound, and complex sentences Questions and statements and commands Facts and assumptions *This happened/this may happen* Modifying verbs expressing possibilities: *might, may* Linking adverbs (*furthermore*) and prepositional phrases (*in addition*) Alternative adverbs (*instead, otherwise*), prepositional phrases (*on the other hand*), and conjunctions (*either, or*) Cause-and-effect adverbs (*then, since*) and conjunctions (*if, so*) Summarizing adverbs (*therefore*) and prepositional phrases (*in conclusion*) Comparison prepositions (*like*) and phrases (*different from*) Personal pronouns (*you*) Visual elements and slogans (*advertisements*)	All necessary punctuation All necessary capitalization Paragraphing

(Continued on following page)

Figure 17 (Continued from previous page)

Activities at the Point of Writing

Explore fiction (*Lester and Clyde, Lester and Clyde Running Scared* [Reece 1976, 1995]) to develop shared knowledge

Undertake research (inquiry): books, Internet, newspaper editorials, articles, and letters to the editor, advertisements

Set up discussion groups

Go on field trips (to wetlands, for example)

Ask a journalist to visit the class and talk about his or her experiences

Use plan sheets

Innovate on an advertisement

List current issues from newspapers

Provide examples of suitable articles and letters to the editor as models

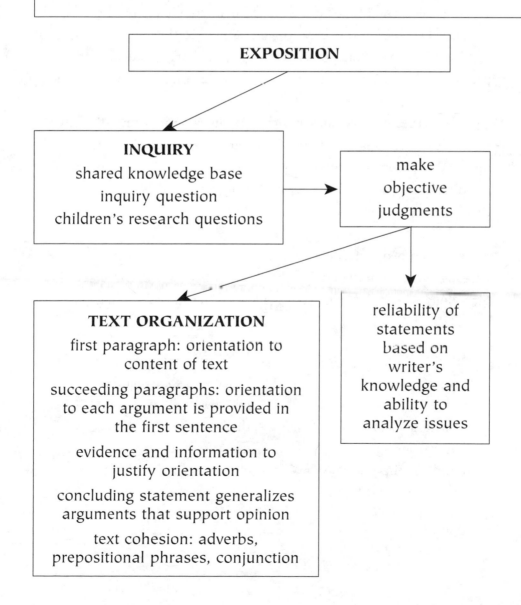

EXPOSITION

INQUIRY
shared knowledge base
inquiry question
children's research questions

make
objective
judgments

TEXT ORGANIZATION

first paragraph: orientation to content of text

succeeding paragraphs: orientation to each argument is provided in the first sentence

evidence and information to justify orientation

concluding statement generalizes arguments that support opinion

text cohesion: adverbs, prepositional phrases, conjunction

reliability of statements based on writer's knowledge and ability to analyze issues

Newspapers are full of exposition: advertisements, editorials, articles, essays, book reviews, movie reviews, play reviews, and letters to the editor. Letters to the editor vary enormously in the way language is used and ideas are arranged, but there are conventions to follow. Point out to students that any letter to the editor must be brief and to the point (most newspapers ask that they not be longer than 175 words), stating the writer's opinion concisely and explaining why she or he holds that view.

Lead-In: Persuasive Fiction

➻ The Lester and Clyde books, by James Reece, are a great way to stimulate opinions and discussions about the effects of pollution on wildlife. Lester and Clyde are frogs living an idyllic life until their environment becomes unsafe because "man's messed this up." They ask, "[Why do] men pollute ponds and foul up the air?" Students can role-play being Lester and Clyde and experience their predicament of living in a polluted environment.

The stories balance humor with a deadly serious theme. The rhyming verse is engaging, and the illustrations capture the characters' feelings and reactions in a humorous way. On the other hand, the stories are filled with emotive language and images that let the reader know this is a serious topic.

➻ When people feel passionately about an issue, they use emotive language. The Lester and Clyde books are filled with clean images and dirty images. List those images together during shared writing.

CLEAN IMAGES	DIRTY IMAGES
far away from the city	peace was soon shattered
in the green countryside	massive steel jaws
sparkling clear	thick smoke
natural springs	unnatural hue
pond supplies their needs	chimneys cast shadows
water clear and bright	"man's messed this up"
lush, idyllic sight	weird and blue

Clean Images (cont'd)	Dirty Images	143
clean pond	toxic waste . . . ozone damage	*Persuasion*
a human child who	awful place	
seems to care	horrible smell	
creatures live without fear	browny, thick muck	
bright	sludge	
peaceful and still	slush	
air is sweet-smelling	old, rotting rubbish and	
surrounded by flowers	mildewy mush	
butterflies flutter	gross human habits	
birds trill	greasy black oil	
	pollution-spoiled pond	

➺ Have students examine how some emotive words are repeated to emphasize a point and how words or phrases relate to the senses.

Inquiry

➺ Now that the class has been stimulated by Lester and Clyde's experiences, begin a study on frogs living in manmade environments. The significant, open-ended questions could be *Are frogs endangered? Can people help them?* Select information that is suitable for your class' learning needs. As you read various pieces of information to the students, they can ask any questions that come to mind. List them on a class chart. For example:

> What are the reasons frogs die?
> Is it true that where frogs live waterways are clean?
> How can people help frogs?
> Do frogs live in manmade environments?

At the end of the week, have the class prioritize the questions and then have pairs read related information to answer one to four questions and record the answers in their journals.

Eventually you will ask each pair to create an advertisement that brings to the attention of readers how frogs are endangered and how people can help. For an example, see Figure 18.

Before students create their own advertisements, they should study the structure and language features of advertisements.

Figure 18

Advertisement

An advertisement presents a strong point of view, but that point of view is not necessarily supported by proven evidence. An advertisement begins with an opening statement or question to attract attention, followed by a series of arguments or recommendations urging the public to purchase certain goods or services or promoting certain activities.

➡ Look at a variety of advertisements and ask these questions:

What are the characteristics of a good advertisement?
What is the function of a good advertisement?

As children explore advertisements, help them see that an advertisement uses emotive and evocative language and is structured to make the reader take notice.

Use the following structure/language example:

TEXT STRUCTURE	PERSUASIVE LANGUAGE
Provide an opener	
Make a statement that	
attracts attention	A Fishes Pen is the electronic pen for you!
or	*or*

Pose a question in the reader's mind	Do you have difficulty sending messages to other fish?
Argue the case	
Personalize the message	A Fishes Pen will solve all your troubles.
Repeat the product's name	
Make an exaggerated and probably unfounded claim	Millions of fish send messages using Fishes Pens.
Point out ease of use	Simply place a Fishes Pen in your mouth and vibrate it up and down. Other fish will get your message.
Sum up/make a recommendation	
Create a feeling of urgency	Be the first to buy a Fishes Pen and send your electronic vibrations, before other schools of fish catch on.
Finish with a positive message	All smart fish will be using Fishes Pens!
Provide purchasing details	Available at Jetty Fish Suppliers

➡ During shared writing, you could innovate on the Fishes Pen advertisement or project some other advertisement on which to innovate. Place a blank transparency over the text you want to change and make the changes on that. (Remember, you can also use a famous person's name to promote the product.)

➡ After showing lots of examples of advertisements and innovating on and writing advertisements with children, have them plan, write, and design their own advertisements. These are things they can advertise:

- Issues
- Products
- Books
- Places to visit
- Films, plays, or events to attend

Have them use the Advertisement Plan (BLM 33, page 146) to help create their ads.

ADVERTISEMENT PLAN

BLM 33

Use this plan to create ideas about your advertisement.

First think about what you want to advertise: _____

Then, think about how you will write your advertisement:

TEXT STRUCTURE	LANGUAGE YOU WILL USE
Provide an opener Make a statement that will attract attention or Pose a question in the reader's mind	
Argue the case Personalize the message	
Repeat the product's name	
Make an exaggerated and probably unfounded claim	
Point out ease of use	
Use a famous person's name to promote the product (optional)	
Sum up/offer a recommendation Convey a feeling of urgency	
Finish with a positive message	

Letter to the Editor

A letter to the editor is generally a response to a situation previously reported or being debated in the newspaper. The writer has been stimulated by the debate or has a concern related to the event. The letter begins with a concise opening statement that expresses agreement or concern, generally from a single point of view. The writer then gives reasons, offers examples, and/or recommends a solution.

➡ Introduce this genre by cutting out letters to the editor from newspapers and magazines and asking students to read them in connection with the following checklist:

Read a letter to the editor. Read the letter again and as you do, check off the elements that are included.

- It begins with a personal opinion about an issue or a reported situation:
  - The writer agrees or disagrees.
  - The writer expresses a concern.
- It states the key point(s) in a way that is easy to understand.
- It provides evidence and information that supports the writer's point of view.
- It offers the writer's recommendation about how the problem can be solved.
- The writer elaborates on this recommendation.
- It concludes with a general statement.

If the writer is answering a previously published letter or reacting to an article, see whether these elements are included.

- In the first lines, the writer states the *headline* or *topic* and the author of the letter, report, or article to which she or he is responding and the *date* it was published.
- The writer indicates agreement or disagreement with the earlier point of view.

➡ In shared sessions, project transparencies of two or three letters to the editor written in response to the same topic. Compare the writers' responses. For example, perhaps a newspaper recently reported on an increase of crime in the city and the fact that people feel unsafe. There were sensational headlines (*Man attacked by knife-wielding youths*) and sensational pictures of youths being frisked by police.

One writer's response:

HEADLINE	MOST WANT A CITY THAT IS SAFE
Text orientation: *Personal viewpoint*	The wishes of the majority who use the city for employment, shopping, and entertainment are very clear. They want a city that is safe for them and where they won't be hassled by . . .
Paragraph orientation:	The city council is unable to take any action . . .
Information to support point of view	It allowed too many nightclubs in the same area . . .
Paragraph orientation: *Elaboration on recommendation*	The state government should . . .
Concluding statement:	Make entry into the city a privilege, not a right.

Show children how the last statement, the writer's opinion, could provoke further argument about the issue. Then look at another writer's response:

HEADLINE	VOICE OF REASON
Text orientation: *Personal viewpoint*	I congratulate [person's name] for being the voice of reason concerning the police operations in the city . . . It looked like a TV drama . . .
Paragraph orientation:	. . . because they are youths, they cannot be searched for weapons because a member of the public suspects. . . .
Information to support point of view	I saw youths chatting in a group . . .
Paragraph orientation: *Elaboration on recommendation*	A twenty-four hour police booth . . . This booth could be . . .

During shared writing, write the missing parts of the previous examples.

149

Persuasion

➡ Discuss a school issue. In a class meeting raise a general issue like what should be done about discarded plastic wrappers in the schoolyard. Then have students write emails or letters to the principal presenting their point of view along with arguments to support it. Have them plan their letter using the outline in BLM 34 (page 150).

Article

➡ Read lots of topical articles in newspapers, magazines, and journals and select good examples to model on an overhead. Point out how an article is organized and the language that is used.

Discuss how the first paragraph orientates the reader to the content. Each succeeding argument forms a new paragraph. Each paragraph includes an orientation to the argument (the first sentence) and evidence and information to support a point of view (the following sentences). A concluding paragraph succinctly ties the arguments together, reinforces the point of view, and perhaps offers a recommendation.

TITLE	WE ALL DESERVE ACCESS TO JUSTICE
Paragraph 1: orientation	Many thousands of people do not have the money to hire a lawyer to represent them. Governments must fund legal aid.
Paragraph 2: orientation supporting information	I will be encouraging lawyers to help with the current situation. But this is a short-term solution until government funding is increased for legal aid.
Paragraph 3: orientation supporting evidence	A litigant wrote a defense argument but did not know the relevant law. It was a sincere effort, but I deemed it necessary to say something about each of the arguments. It took me almost a week. If the litigant had been represented by a lawyer, I am sure the matter could have been dealt with in a few hours.

LETTER TO THE EDITOR (OR PRINCIPAL) PLAN

BLM 34

Use key words and phrases to plan your letter before you write it:

Headline

Opening statement (the issue)

Where I stand on the issue (my point of view/opinion—am I *for* or *against*?)

Arguments to support my point of view (evidence/information)

Recommendations

Concluding statement/summary

Paragraph 4: orientation supporting information	I believe people must be provided with basic legal information and advice.
Paragraph 5: orientation supporting information	*Next,* access to courts should be made easier . . .
Paragraph 6: orientation supporting information	*The next task* is to expand . . .
Paragraph 7: orientation supporting information	*Finally,* there is a need for . . .
Concluding statement (reflects opening statement)	Let us join together with governments to close the gap in access to justice.

—Based on an article written by John Harber Phillips
(chief justice of Victoria, Australia)

➼ As students research an issue, have them write the relevant key words and phrases on the Persuasive Article Plan (BLM 35, page 152).

Assessment: Learning Outcomes Profile

Assess each student's writing by examining it in connection with the achievements listed on the Persuasive Exposition Learning Outcomes Profile (BLM 36, page 153) and entering either a check mark or an explanation on the form. For example:

Write an advertisement	√ *great drawings*
Create a headline to capture interest	√

You can also write general comments about the student's overall performance.

PERSUASIVE ARTICLE PLAN

BLM 35

While researching the issue, write key words or phrases under the appropriate headings.

The headline is:

First paragraph: (orientation to the issue)

Paragraph 2:
(orientation) *To begin with . . .*

(evidence, information to support view)

Paragraph 3:
(orientation) *Another argument . . .*

(evidence, information to support view)

Paragraph 4:
(orientation) *A solution could be . . .*

(recommendation)

Paragraph 5: (concluding statement)
(generalizes the orientation; returns to main point of argument)

Finally . . .

PERSUASIVE EXPOSITION LEARNING OUTCOMES PROFILE
for parents and other teachers

Name _____

Has been studying persuasive exposition and is now able to:

Text

Select a topic _____

Read, research, and extract relevant information _____

Write an advertisement _____

Write a letter to the editor _____

Write an article _____

Maintain a point of view _____

Contextual Understanding

Take a position based on the information known _____

Offer recommendations _____

Distinguish between fact and assumption _____

Proofread and make corrections _____

Text and Language Structures

Create a headline to capture interest _____

Sequence the information:

   ■ Orient reader to content and context _____

   ■ Provide evidence and information _____

   ■ State argument _____

   ■ Give a short concluding statement that sums up argument _____

Link paragraphs using adverbs and prepositions _____

Link sentences using conjunctions _____

Use modifying verbs to express possibilities _____

Use common nouns

Use emotive language

Conventions

Use all relevant capitalization _____

Use all relevant punctuation _____

Use paragraphs

Additional Comments

_____

_____

Notes

Argument and Counterargument

Argument and counterargument argues a case from two perspectives in order to sway readers toward a particular point of view.

Argument and counterargument requires higher levels of thinking and more formal, explicit language. In it, students immerse themselves in an issue: they read, discuss, note important information, and ask questions. They make judgments, clarify their point of view, and argue for and against a particular stance. Then they conclude by recommending one of the points of view.

Like the other expository genres, argument is based on inquiry:

- You raise a significant, open-ended question.
- Students ask subordinate questions and use them to direct their investigation and research and develop opinions.

Students also learn how to use counterarguments to reinforce their case: *It has been said that . . . , but the flaw in that argument is . . .*
There are four steps to understanding how to write an argument:

- Debate for and against an issue orally.
- As a class, deconstruct examples of the genre.
- Have students, in pairs, reassemble cutup, jumbled paragraphs.
- Let students discuss why they have reconstructed the paragraphs as they have.

ARGUMENT/COUNTERARGUMENT PROGRAM PLAN

Figure 19

Argument/counterargument (extending+ writers)		
Content		
Researching a contemporary issue (inquiry), isolating the main points, and taking a position (could also be an historical issue) Stating a point of view in a way that seeks to change the reader's opinion or attitude Justifying the position on the basis of evidence (both fact and supposition) Presenting differing points of view (arguments *for* and *against*) to reinforce a particular point of view		
Text Structures	**Language Structures**	**Conventions:**
One persuasive point of view	Technical words	All necessary punctuation
Headline to capture interest	Mostly impersonal voice	
Concise orientation so readers can predict what the piece is about	Emotive language	All necessary capitalization
	Mixture of simple, compound, and complex sentences	Paragraphing
Sequenced argument: orientation (focus) followed by justification (evidence, information)	Questions, statements, and commands Facts and assumptions *This happened/this may happen* Modal verbs expressing possibilities: *might, may*	
Counterargument (reasons for and against; taking two perspectives)		
Concluding statement: summing up and making a recommendation	Linking adverbs (*furthermore*) and prepositional phrases (*in addition*) Alternative adverbs (*instead, otherwise*), prepositional phrases (*on the other hand*), and conjunctions (*either, or*) Cause-and-effect adverbs (*then, since*) and conjunctions (*if, so*) Summarizing adverbs (*therefore*) and prepositional phrases (*in conclusion*) Comparison prepositions (*like*) and phrases (*different from*)	

Lead-In

➥ Begin by sharing *Viewpoints on Waste*, by Rodney Martin (1993), a nonfiction book that presents different points of view about waste.

Examine the cover and discuss the different types of packaging shown. Ask students to list some types of waste.

Point out that the author of the book interviewed six different people who have varied roles in the community (a plastics manufacturer, a Greenpeace spokesperson, some residents).

Also point out the organizational headings *Problems with Waste*, *Solutions*, *Facts About Waste*, and *Ideas*.

➥ Immerse students in the topic by taking a field trip to a recycling plant or showing appropriate films, videos, and art prints.

➥ Identify a significant, open-ended question—*Is waste necessary?*—and ask students to form two teams to debate the issue, with each team taking a different perspective. One team will speak for the plastics manufacturers, who say they are providing employment, and the other will present the moral opposition to waste promoted by groups like Greenpeace.

Before they debate, team members can explore resources and ideas and list questions and comments (in their journals or on a class chart) about things they need to understand in order to conduct the debate effectively:

What is waste?
What is pollution?
How is waste disposed of in our society?
What problems does waste cause in our society?

Organization

➤ Prepare and discuss the following chart, which children can refer to when writing their argument:

Alternating Arguments and Counterarguments

First paragraph: orientation to content (stated concisely)

Succeeding paragraphs:
opening sentence stating point of view/argument
further sentences justifying the point of view/argument

Concluding paragraph: sums up arguments and takes a position

Example: Text Deconstruction and Reconstruction

Display the following open-ended question:

Does logging affect our environment?

On an overhead, deconstruct an example of a written argument. Focus on one or two elements at a time. (The following example has been adapted from *Teaching ESL Through Science* [Australia Department of Education 1998].)

Heading   The Impact of Logging Forests

First paragraph: content orientation (impersonal voice)
The logging of rain forests has caused major conflicts between environmental groups around the world and countries that want to increase their export income by expanding their timber industry. Clearly, there are very different views on whether or not the logging of rain forests has a major impact on our environment.

Paragraph 2: first sentence (beginning with a prepositional phrase) introduces an argument; second sentence justifies it

To begin, major logging companies argue that logging of forests is essential in providing the products we use daily. These companies claim that if there were no logging of rain forests, there would not be sufficient timber for building and for the production of paper.

Paragraph 3: first sentence (beginning with an adverb) introduces a counterargument; second sentence justifies it

However, many indigenous peoples who rely on the forests for shelter and food claim that they have had to move into cities because there are no trees left to sustain their way of life. Some of these indigenous cultures are being wiped out as we destroy their homes to build our own.

Paragraph 4: first sentence (beginning with a prepositional phrase) introduces a counterargument; remaining sentences justify it

At the same time, it is argued that logging has resulted in benefits for all, including the indigenous people. The cleared forests make land available for cattle and crop farming, which provide people with meat, cereals, and other food products. The opportunities for food exports **may** result in an increase in employment and financial gain.

modifier

Paragraph 5: first sentence (beginning with an adverb) introduces a counterargument; remaining sentences justify it

Nevertheless, the increased wealth from the cleared land appears to be short lived, and the profits go to the major logging companies, not the people who live in the forests. The forest's soil is so weak in nutrients that it takes a large area to raise enough beef to make a living. It is **probable** that the beef is not eaten locally but exported. A further long-term disadvantage is that clearing land can change the local climate and cause droughts, massive floods, erosion, or degradation of the topsoil.

modifier

Paragraph 6: first sentence (beginning with an adjective) introduces an argument; remaining sentences justify it

Another argument is that some logging companies have reforestation programs. They believe forests can grow back to their original state and that the accompanying wildlife will flourish again. This **may** happen, but can people replace the life forms that have been damaged as a result of deforestation? It has been shown in the past that it is impossible to replace the varied life forms of a forest.

modifier

Summary paragraph: conclusion

In summary, current evidence suggests that the long-term disadvantages of logging—**possible** extinction of native fauna and flora and degradation of land—outweigh the short-term advantages and, for this reason, the practice must be banned before more irreversible damage is done to our environment.

modifier

Have children reconstruct the text:

➥ Cut each argument paragraph into three parts: the phrase (or word) beginning the paragraph, the first sentence introducing the argument, and the justification. For example:

> it is argued that logging has resulted in benefits for all, including the indigenous people.

> At the same time,

> The cleared forests make land available for cattle and crop farming, which provide people with meat, cereals, and other food products. The opportunities for food exports may result in an increase in employment and financial gain.

Divide the class into five groups. Give each group the cutup paragraphs to reassemble. Have them discuss the following:

> Which sentence introduces the argument?
> What language links one paragraph to the next?
> What sentences justify the argument?

➡ Cut up each paragraph and have the class reassemble them in order. Have them discuss the following:

> Which paragraph orients the reader to the content?
> Which paragraphs introduce arguments and counterarguments?
> Which paragraph is the concluding statement?

➡ Additional issues students could investigate and write arguments for and against:

> Should we keep animals in zoos? (You could begin by reading *Should There Be Zoos?* by Tony Stead [2002].)
> Should whales be hunted as exotic food?
> Why advertise? Are advertisements worth the money? Do they annoy? Are they enjoyable? What do they say about our society?
> Is it important to change house designs? (Consider heating and cooling factors and areas in which tornados and earthquakes occur.)

Forming Points of View, Planning, and Writing

➡ As students research their topics, give them a copy of BLM 37 (page 162), which they can use to help them form points of view.

FORMING A POINT OF VIEW PLAN SHEET

Name _____

As you read, list your questions.

The focus is the point you are making for or against.

You also need to list evidence to support that point.

Issue: _____

Questions: _____

_____

_____

_____

_____

Argument for	Argument against
Focus:	Focus:
Evidence, information:	Evidence, information:
Focus:	Focus:
Evidence, information:	Evidence, information:
Focus:	Focus:
Evidence, information:	Evidence, information:

My opinion is:

➥ After they have formed their points of view, they can plan their arguments using the graphic organizer in BLM 43 (page 173) or the Inspiration® computer program. Then they can use their plans to write their final articles or essays.

Language Structures

When children begin writing, they use simple sentences (*I went to town*). They learn about capitalization and basic punctuation (periods, question marks, exclamation points, quotation marks). They add descriptive adjectives and adverbs. They learn to make compound sentences by joining sentences with simple conjunctions (*and, but*). They start composing simple paragraphs (the beginning, the middle, and the end).

Then they move on to more complex language structures: subordinate clauses, connectives, adverbial and prepositional phrases, commas, semicolons, and colons, and separate paragraphs for each new idea. They use words to link ideas from one paragraph to the next and learn about the conditional nature of assumptions.

Planned activities that reinforce language structures generally happen in small groups in which the students interact with one another and the teacher. Figure 20 shows some explicit ways to teach children essential facets of the language. (Small whiteboards or chalkboards are ideal for hypothesizing and practicing. Knowing that attempts that don't work out can be easily erased allows children to take risks they might not take on paper.)

Assessment: Learning Outcomes Profile

Assess each student's writing by examining it in connection with the achievements listed on the Argument and Counterargument Learning Outcomes Profile (BLM 38, page 167) and entering either a check mark or an explanation on the form. For example:

> Write an argument and counterargument √
> Orient reader to content and context √

You can also write general comments about the student's overall performance.

Figure 20

Language Stuctures and Reinforcing Activities

Clauses, complex sentences

A **main clause** is a group of words with a *subject* (the actor) and a *verb* (the action). Main clauses can exist on their own: *The boy jumped high.* A compound sentence has at least two main clauses linked by a conjunction (*and, but*): *The boy jumped high, and he won the competition.*

A **subordinate clause** cannot exist on its own: *The boy jumped high* (main clause) *when he came to the puddle* (subordinate clause).

Activities to reinforce the use of complex sentences:

➻ Experiment with different ways sentences can be written: simple form, compound form, complex form. (Distinguish them by writing each kind in a different-colored ink.)

➻ Combine three short clauses into compound or complex sentences.

➻ Manipulate sentences manually or on the computer.

Connective adverbs

organize the text: *alternatively, moreover, then, finally, suddenly*

join clauses: *meanwhile, then, so, besides, when*

join paragraphs or sentences: *likewise, meanwhile, therefore, however, previously*

Activities to reinforce the use of adverbs:

➻ String out a clothesline and give clothespins and word cards to the students so they can manipulate sentences containing adverbs:

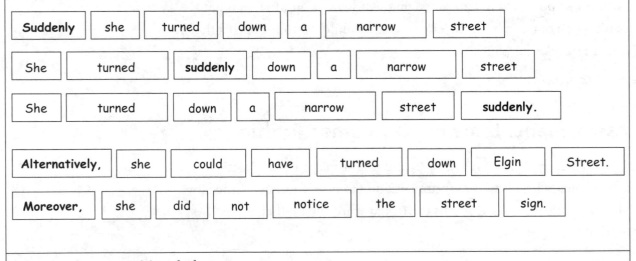

Connective prepositional phrases

organize the text: *in addition, on the other hand, at the same time, to this end, in the night*

join clauses: *in spite of, in case*

join paragraphs or sentences: *in contrast, to this end*

An activity to reinforce the use of prepositional phrases*

➥ Show the effect different prepositions have on the word *night*:

In the night . . .
During the night . . .
Throughout the night . . .

Show how prepositional phrases can begin a response:

In my opinion . . .

Show how prepositional phrases can counter an argument:

On the other hand . . .

Conjunctions

join clauses: *or, whereas, if, because, although, unless, while, like, also*

join paragraphs or sentences: *otherwise, yet*

An activity to reinforce the use of conjunctions*

➥ Give students paper, scissors, and a pocket chart and the below story map. Have them create a story using the map and conjunctions written on cards: *so, if, because, while, since, though, when*

Who: The Three Bears and a Wolf

When: Mother Bear made some porridge for Father Bear and Baby Bear

Ending: The Wolf ran away howling

Comma

The **comma** is an important organizational tool in more complex material. Children begin learning to use commas by writing lists.

Commas are also used when writing

- subordinate clauses: *Although it was dark, he rode his bike home.*
- connectives (adverbs, prepositional phrases): *Alternatively, he . . .   In addition, she . . .*

Write sentences and cut separately, phrases, adverbs, and commas. Students in pairs discuss and reassemble the sentences.

| Although it was dark | , | he rode his bike home |

| Alternatively | , | he could have | read his favorite book |

(Continued from previous page)

Paragraphs

Paragraphing allows the writer to build on ideas; each new paragraph discusses a new idea.

Activities to reinforce the use of paragraphs*

➤ Write a paragraph and cut it up into sentences. Have children reconstruct the paragraph.

➤ Divide a page into four boxes. Write a heading in each box that introduces a new idea. Have children expand on each heading. Boxes help children visualize when text moves from one idea to the next.

> Humpty Dumpty sat on the wall

It was a hot day. Humpty sat on a wall for hours gazing at the uniformed troops. He was feeling on top of the world. He leaned forward and punched the air with his clenched fist.

> Humpty Dumpty had a great fall

Suddenly, his rounded body began to rock . . .

> All the king's horses and all the king's men couldn't put Humpty together again

Cautiously, the soldiers broke rank. They huddled around . . .

(*Adapted from London Department for Education and Employment 2000)

ARGUMENT AND COUNTERARGUMENT
LEARNING OUTCOMES PROFILE
for parents and other teachers

Name _____

Has been studying argument and counterargument and is now able to:

Text
Write an argument/counterargument _____

Contextual Understanding
Select a topic _____
Read, research, and extract relevant information _____
Take a position based on the information known _____
Distinguish between argument and counterargument _____
Offer recommendations _____
Distinguish between fact and assumption_____
Proofread and make corrections _____

Text and Language Structures _____
Create a headline to capture interest _____
Sequence information
  Orient reader to content and context _____
  Provide evidence and information _____
  State arguments and counterarguments _____
  Give a short concluding statement that
    sums up arguments and takes a position _____
Link paragraphs using adverbs and prepositions
  (*also, however, in*) _____
Link sentences using conjunctions (*because, although*)_____
Use modal verbs to express possibilities (*might, may*) _____

Conventions
Use all relevant and appropriate capitalization _____
Use all relevant and appropriate punctuation _____
Use paragraphs _____

Additional Comments

_____
_____
_____

LANGUAGE STRUCTURE – WRITING GENRES

Level	1	2	3	4	5
A an	X	X	X	X	X
Adjectives, + phrases, + of degree (comparative, superlative)	A	X	XXX	X+	X+
Adverbs, + of degree			X	XX	X+
Affixes – suffixes, +prefixes		A	XX	X+	X+
Alliteration	X	X	X	X	X
Analogy			X	X	X
Apostrophes – missing letter, + sing. possessive, + plural possessive		XA	XX	XXX	X+
Brackets (parenthesis)					X
Bullet points					X
Capitalization	X	X	X	X	X
Commands		X	X	X	X
Commas – lists, + joining clauses, + before direct speech, + interjections, + connectives		XA	XXX	XXXX	XXXXX
Complex sentences				X	X
Compound sentences	A	X	X	X	X
Conjunctions	A	X	X	X	X
Connectives			X	X	X
Direct speech	A	X	X	X	X
Exclamation marks	A	X	X	X	X
Grammatical agreement	A	X	X	X	X
Metaphor				A	X
Nouns – common, + proper, + collective, + plurals		XXAX	XXXX	X+	X+
Paragraphing		A	X	X	X
Periods	X	X	X	X	X
Pluralization / Singular	X	X	X	X	X
Prepositions - + phrases			X	XX	X+
Pronouns - + plurals		X	X	XX	X+
Question Marks	A	X	X	X	X
Questions / Statements	A	X	X	X	X
Reported speech				X	X
Simple sentences	X	X	X	X	X
Speech marks	A	X	X	X	X
Subordinate clauses					X
Verbs - regular tense,+ +irregular tense, +auxiliary, + modals, + plurals	XA	XXX	XXXXX	X+	X+

A – refer to the skill only
X – plan, teach skill

Generic Blackline Masters
GENERIC PROGRAM PLAN

BLM 39

_____ **Program Plan**
Content

Text Structures	**Language Structures**	**Conventions**

Activities at the Point of Writing

LEARNING OUTCOMES PROFILE
for parents and other teachers

GENRE: _____

Name _____

Has been studying _____ and is now able to:

Text

Contextual Understanding

Conventions

Additional Comments

WRITING CONFERENCE RECORD

BLM 41

NAME:

Date: *Teaching Focus:*

Discussion points:

Student's writing goals:

Date: *Teaching Focus:*

Discussion points:

Student's writing goals:

Date: *Teaching Focus:*

Discussion points:

Student's writing goals:

Date: *Teaching Focus:*

Discussion points:

Student's writing goals:

Date: *Teaching Focus:*

Discussion points:

Student's writing goals:

Date: *Teaching Focus:*

Discussion points:

Student's writing goals:

STORY JIGSAW

BLM 42

Write the main story in the jigsaw: how the story began, who the characters were, what happened, and how the story ended. Cut out the jigsaw pieces. Reassemble the jigsaw.

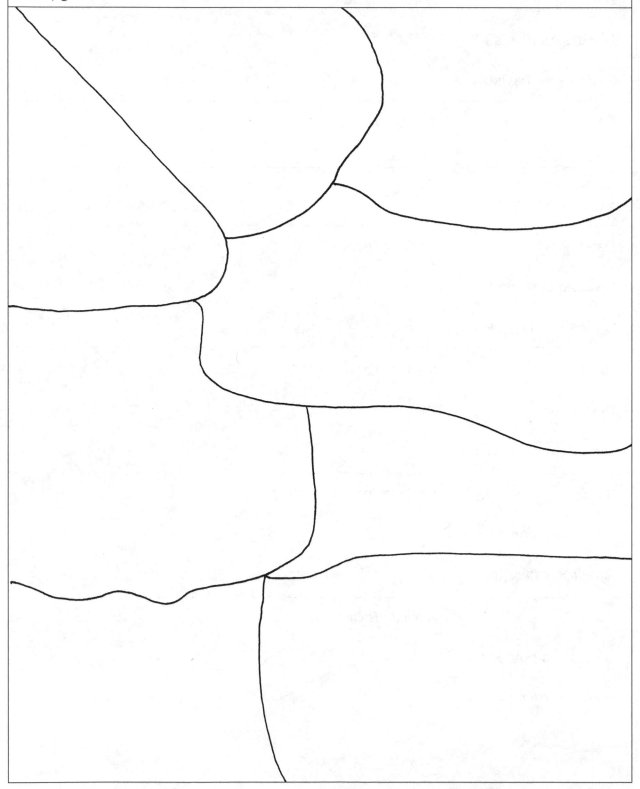

BLM 43

Annotate and cut out the shapes as you plan each part of your piece.

Paste each element onto a sheet in the order you will use it.

Ahlberg, Janet, and Allan Ahlberg. 1990. *The Jolly Postman, or, Other People's Letters.* New York: Little, Brown.

Animal Facts Series. Various authors and dates. Rigby PM Collection. Barrington, IL: Rigby Education.

Anstey, Michelle. 1986. "Connecting Writing and Reading." In *Writing and Reading to Learn,* ed. Nea Stewart-Dore. Newtown, NSW, Australia: Primary English Teaching Association.

Australia Department of Education, Curriculum Resources. 1998. *Teaching ESL Through Science: A Science Curriculum for Intensive English Language Programs.* Adelaide, SA, Australia: Australia Department of Education.

Barrs, Myra. 2000. "The Reader in the Writer." *Reading* 34 (2).

Brian, J., and G. Pascoe. 1992. *There Was a Big Fish: Limericks.* Adelaide, SA, Australia: Era.

Bright, Michael. 1987. *Pollution and Wildlife.* London: Franklin Watts.

Carle, Eric. 1975. *The Very Hungry Caterpillar.* New York: Penguin Putnam.

Christelow, Eileen. 1991. *Five Little Monkeys Jumping on the Bed.* New York: Houghton Mifflin.

Croser, Josephine. 1996. *Whale Watching.* Vernon Hills, IL: ETA/Cuisenaire.

———. 2000. *The Universe.* Our World Series. Adelaide, SA, Australia: Era Magic Bean.

Curriculum Corporation. 1994. *A Statement of English for Australian Schools.* Melbourne, VIC, Australia: Curriculum Corporation.

Dahl, Roald. 1998. *The Magic Finger.* Reprint. New York: Penguin Puffin.

Daniels, Harvey. 1994. *Literature Circles: Voice and Choice in the Student-Centered Classroom.* York, ME: Stenhouse.

Dillon, Franca, and Melena Cahill. 1991. *Key into Literacy.* Melbourne, VIC, Australia: Longman Cheshire.

Dodd, Lynley. 2001. *Hairy Maclary from Donald's Dairy.* Berkley, CA: Tricycle.

DSP Literacy Project. 1988. *Teaching Factual Writing: A Genre-Based Approach.* Sydney, NSW, Australia: NSW Department of Social Education.

Ekman, Jean Adams. 2001. *Clarence and the Great Surprise.* Flagstaff, AZ: Northland.

Fox, Mem. 1996. *Zoo-Looking.* New York: Mondo.

Galdone, Paul. 1979. *The Three Billy Goats Gruff.* Boston: Clarion Books.

George, Jean Craighead. 1997. *Everglades.* New York: HarperCollins.

Graham, Amanda. 1991. *Cinderella/Alex and the Glass Slipper.* Adelaide, SA, Australia: Era.

Grobler, Piet. 2002. *Hey, Frog!* Asheville, NC: Front Street; Rotterdam, Netherlands: Lemniscaat.

Hamster, J., and K. Murdoch. 2000. *Planning Integrated Units of Work for Social Educators.* Melbourne, VIC, Australia: Eleanor Curtain.

Hill, Susan. 1991. *Poems Not to Be Missed.* Adelaide, SA, Australia: Era.

Inspiration® (education edition). Inspiration® Software, Portland, OR.

Johansen, Iris. 1996. *The Ugly Duckling.* New York: Bantam Dell/Random House.

Jorgensen, Gail. 1988. *On a Dark and Scary Night.* Melbourne, VIC, Australia: Macmillan.

Kid Pix.® Broderbund Software/Riverdeep. Novato, CA, and Hiawatha, IA.

Kidspiration® (education edition). Inspiration® Software, Portland, OR.

London Department for Education and Employment. 2000. *The National Literacy Strategy: Grammar for Writing.* London: London Department for Education and Employment.

Maestro, Betsy, and Giulio Maestro. 1989. *The Story of the Statue of Liberty.* New York: HarperTrophy.

Marshall, James. 1998. *George and Martha 'Round and 'Round*. Boston: Houghton Mifflin.

Martin, Bill Jr. 1992. *Brown Bear, Brown Bear, What Do You See?* New York: Henry Holt.

Martin, Judith A. 1998. *Monsieur Armand*. Adelaide, SA, Australia: Era.

Martin, Rodney. 1993. *Viewpoints on Waste*. In-Fact Series. Adelaide, SA, Australia: Era Magic Bean.

McCafferty, Catherine. 2002. *The Gingerbread Man*. American Education Publishing Inc.

Microsoft® Publisher 97. Microsoft Corporation, Redmond, WA.

Microsoft® Word 2000. Microsoft Corporation, Redmond, WA.

Moore, Inga. 1997. *Six-Dinner Sid*. Vernon Hills, IL: ETA/Cuisenaire.

Pascoe, Gwen. 1994a. *Deep in a Rainforest*. Vernon Hills, IL: ETA/Cuisenaire.

———. 1994b. *One Wobbly Wheelbarrow*. Vernon Hills, IL: ETA/Cuisenaire.

Pfister, Marcus. 1995. *The Rainbow Fish*. New York: North-South.

Phillips, John. 2000. "St. James Ethics Center's Annual Lawyers Lecture." Edited. *The Australian* 11 April, 13 (Opinion page).

Pollock, Yvonne. 1995. *Old Man's Mitten*. New York: Mondo.

Reece, James. 1976. *Lester and Clyde*. New York: Scholastic Paperbacks.

———. 1995. *Lester and Clyde Running Scared*. New York: Scholastic Paperbacks.

Robinson, Claire. 2001. *Elephants*. In the Wild Series. Chicago: Heinemann Library.

Romay, Saturnino. 1994. *Birds on Stage*. New York: Scholastic: Wiggleworks

Rose, Gerald. 1975. *Trouble in the Ark*. Harrisburg, PA: Morehouse.

Schaffer, Frank. 1988. *Fairy Tale Sequencing: Visual Sequencing Cards*. Palo Verdes, CA: Frank Schaffer.

Short, Kathy, Carolyn Burke, and Jerome Harste. 1996. *Creating Classrooms for Authors and Inquirers*. 2d ed. Portsmouth, NH: Heinemann.

Simmonds, Debbie. 1998. *Birds*. 8 vols. In-Fact Series. Adelaide, SA, Australia: Era Magic Bean.

Simon, Liz. 2004. *Strategic Spelling: Every Writer's Tool*. Portsmouth, NH: Heinemann.

Stead, Tony. 2002. *Should There Be Zoos?* New York: Mondo.

Taback, Simms. 1997. *There Was an Old Lady Who Swallowed a Fly.* New York: Viking.

————. 2002. *The House That Jack Built.* New York: Viking.

Topping, Keith, et al. 2000. "Paired Writing: A Framework for Effective Collaboration." *Reading* 34 (2).

Van Allsburg, Chris. 1981. *Jumanji.* Boston: Houghton Mifflin.

White, E. B. 1974. *Charlotte's Web.* New York: HaperCollins Publishers.

Wild, Margaret. 1993. *Our Granny.* Geneva, IL: Houghton Mifflin.

Winer, Yvonne. 1990. *Helbertia the Vile.* Adelaide, SA, Australia: Era.